rich *in* l♡ve

when God rescues messy people

IRENE GARCIA
WITH LISSA HALLS JOHNSON

David C Cook

transforming lives together

RICH IN LOVE
Published by David C Cook
4050 Lee Vance View
Colorado Springs, CO 80918 U.S.A.

David C Cook Distribution Canada
55 Woodslee Avenue, Paris, Ontario, Canada N3L 3E5

David C Cook U.K., Kingsway Communications
Eastbourne, East Sussex BN23 6NT, England

The graphic circle C logo is a registered trademark of David C Cook.

Unless otherwise noted, all Scripture quotations are taken from the *Holy Bible, New Living Translation*, copyright © 1996, 2007 by Tyndale House Foundation. Used by permission of Tyndale House Publishers, Inc., Carol Stream, Illinois 60188. All rights reserved. Scripture quotations marked NIV are taken from the Holy Bible, New International Version®, NIV®. Copyright © 1973, 2011 by Biblica, Inc.™ Used by permission of Zondervan. All rights reserved worldwide. www.zondervan.com; and NASB are taken from the New American Standard Bible®, Copyright © 1960, 1995 by The Lockman Foundation. Used by permission. (www.Lockman.org.) The epigraph verse on page 7 is a combination of the NIV and NLT.

LCCN 2013953100
ISBN 978-1-4347-0688-1
eISBN 978-0-7814-1126-4

© 2014 Irene Garcia, Lissa Halls Johnson

The Team: Don Pape, John Blase, Nick Lee, Caitlyn Carlson, Karen Athen
Cover Design: Amy Konyndyk
Cover Photo: Daley Hake

Printed in the United States of America
First Edition 2014

1 2 3 4 5 6 7 8 9 10

112613

Domingo, my love,
my life—thank you.

contents

The LORD is merciful and compassionate, slow to anger and rich in love.

Psalm 145:8

the hero

Every story has a hero. Without a hero, there isn't really a story. A true hero—in a story and in real life—is somebody who steps out bravely into a very difficult or frightening situation, who does something that makes the rest of us look on in awe. Heroes perform amazing acts that are not truly required of them, yet they do those things anyway out of a strong moral character. This is the person the story is really about. In our story, God is the hero. Without him, there would be no story.

Our story is messy. We are simple people. We didn't go to college. We didn't learn how to do everything right. As a matter of fact, we did just about everything wrong and out of order.

If I hadn't gotten pregnant at fifteen, I never would have married Domingo. Back then, Domingo was my best friend—until he drank and became someone else, someone mean, quick-tempered, and physically abusive. If God hadn't sent a woman named Mary Barshaw into my life, I wouldn't have stayed married.

While Domingo was a young boy who couldn't control his drinking or his anger, I was a strong-willed girl who would lose control of her tongue. Domingo would get violent; I would get mouthy. Many nights he came home late from drinking and hurt me physically and emotionally. I learned early on I couldn't match him physically, so my words became my weapon. When he was sober again, I made sure to hurt him by spewing the most wicked and vile words I could think of. It gave me an odd sense of satisfaction to be able to pierce him deeply. He broke my nose. I broke his heart.

Now we are nothing like those confused kids who married at sixteen and stumbled a lot on their way through life. We have changed drastically. But someone told me that the darker the darkness, the greater the miracle of change. And because it was nothing short of a miracle that changed us, I am willing to write about the deep darkness that draws attention to the real hero of our story: God.

Not only is our story messy, but the stories of our children are a muddled mess. Yes, we are simple people, but we know one thing: God resurrects the broken things, the things that were dead—a heart, a marriage, a family. He resurrected our children out of the ashes. Out of the horrors in which they grew up. Domingo and I are just the fortunate ones who get to stand and watch in awe as our God works.

Trouble and difficulty often surround us. We are tired and worn-out. We fall on our knees in a dark closet and plead with God for wisdom, for help in caring for so many broken children. And yet we are rich in love. I don't know why, but God chose to bring us these little ones to love and cherish. And how can you say no to God? God's gifts don't always come in ways we expect. But saying yes and accepting his gifts are the only ways for God to be the hero of the story.

PART 1

MERCIFUL

♡

in the beginning

Irene

As a child, I loved my life.

I was born in Hollywood the second of four kids: my sister Billie, then me, Mark, and Marie. Although my father considered himself a full-blooded Mexican, he was born on American soil to a hardworking family. My father worked as the maître d' at Ciro's nightclub in Hollywood, a famous hangout for the biggest stars of the '50s and '60s. Those were the days of Bobby Darin, Sandra Dee, and Frank Sinatra. His job required him to interact with the likes of Lana Turner, Clark Gable, and Marilyn Monroe, as well as some of the more famous mafiosi.

Because of his job, my father worked hard at being Americanized and making sure we were as well. He spoke to us only in English, though my mother—who was Irish Mexican—spoke to us in Spanish. For my father, everything was about education and speaking proper English. He was very strict—he lived by a lot of the old ways. If we did something wrong, we would be punished.

Still, I loved my father very much. He was my biggest cheerleader. My whole life my dad's words to me were "You can do anything you put your mind to, Rene. You're smart. You can do it, Rene." And I believed him.

I also thought he was so handsome. He was a bit of a celebrity among our extended family because of his encounters with famous people. At family gatherings, everyone clustered around to hear him tell his stories about the movie stars he knew.

When my father went to work, he wore either a tuxedo or a black suit and expensive cologne that smelled wonderful. Before walking out the door, he'd bend down and point to his cheek for me to kiss. I treasured our little ritual and eagerly waited for that moment when I would get to kiss his freshly shaven, smooth, yummy-smelling cheek. To this day, my sisters and I still kiss his cheek and say, "Mmmm, Daddy. You smell so good."

In addition to sharing stories about movie stars, he loved to tell how when he met my mom it was love at first sight. He had wanted to marry her right away. And no one doubted that because my mom was a very beautiful woman.

Everyone loved my mother. She had so many family and friends who wanted to be near her. She was kind and the most hospitable woman I have ever met. She cooked the most amazing authentic Mexican food. She liked TV, so it was on all day—I must have watched every old movie ever made. My mom also loved music. Whenever we drove somewhere, the radio was tuned to either a Spanish music station or the oldies.

We spent most of our free time with family. On weekends we might go to East Los Angeles and visit relatives, which meant lots of food and laughter. They'd play Spanish music, and we'd all dance the Mexican cumbia.

When we weren't with extended family, we had great times staying at home. My parents played records, and we'd all dance. My dad was also a gourmet cook, and he often prepared dinner on his days off. I stayed by his side and helped him. As a result, I could cook anything by the time I got married.

As a little girl, I walked to Catholic school every day. I was very proud that I was born to two Catholic parents. The nuns told us that if we were not Catholics we would go to hell. So I knew I was special because I was a Catholic.

The nuns also taught me to fear God, telling me that if I disobeyed I would go to hell. I must admit, they scared the daylights out of me. Still, I feared the Devil more than I feared God, and sometimes I thought I saw the Devil at night. I went to confession as often as I could so I would be forgiven for all the mischief I got into. I believed the priest was someone special, someone who could let me into heaven, so I wanted him to know who I was.

With all my trips to confession, I knew the "Hail Marys" and "Our Fathers" by heart. Somehow, though, I felt like something was wrong with this ritual. How could simple prayers keep me from hell? I wanted so badly to be connected to God but felt I wasn't. Something gnawed at me—there had to be more I needed to do to connect to him.

I really loved God and believed in him, but I was never sure what he thought about me. I would pray on my own and ask God for miracles. One time my grandmother gave me five dollars to make a bunch of octopuses out of yarn for her to sell at a boutique. I blew the money on myself instead. Then I got scared and felt guilty and put an octopus in the closet, praying for God to multiply it. I believed God was capable of anything, so I was very upset when he didn't give me the miracle of multiplied octopuses I'd asked him for.

I don't remember my parents talking to us about God. They sent us to church without them and, as far as I knew, had never set foot inside—except on the day they were married by the church.

One day my dad took me for a ride to a place called the San Fernando Valley. He showed me this brand-new, amazing house with white rocks on top of it and told me we were going to leave Hollywood and move to this new place. I was very excited. I thought this meant we were rich. And then, after we moved, my dad gave us an unbelievable gift. He had a huge pool built in our backyard. I was dumbfounded when I saw how big it was. I knew we were special—we had to be. I didn't know anyone else who had their own pool. We had wonderful summer days when family would come over for swimming and plenty of food.

I felt so secure and happy. Since then I've seen that my mom and dad were not perfect; they kept their personal problems private. Like many children, I lived in a dreamworld and couldn't see the bad in my family. But there are no perfect parents in the world, and mine did what they could with what they had. However, my mom and dad accomplished one very important thing—they gave us a home where we felt safe and secure.

Domingo

Domingo's childhood was as different from mine as night is from day. He was one of ten children in a family of migrant farmworkers who followed the crops from Texas to Minnesota. The "homes" they lived in temporarily were the poorly constructed one-room shacks provided by the farmers. An old station wagon and a trailer held everything his large family owned.

His earliest memory is as a toddler sorting through rocks to find beans his family could cook and eat. As a little guy, he sat on a log so his older brothers could use a two-man saw to cut wood for the woodstove. The stove not only provided heat for the shack but was where his mother cooked their food. Domingo remembers watching his pregnant mom cook and breast-feed at the same time. But the stove didn't provide enough heat. Domingo shivered constantly, getting a clear view of Minnesota's winter snow through the wide gaps in the walls of their picker's shack. A bunch of the kids slept in one bed with clothes piled on top of them as they tried to stay warm.

Once in a while a guy came around selling shaved ice. That's all Domingo wanted—shaved ice. But his family never had the money for even such a simple treat.

My mother-in-law once shared with me that on occasion, his father would go to the local church to preach the Word of God and talk from the pulpit about the hardships of his family. The caring people would take a love offering for his family. He graciously accepted the cash, then went to town to splurge all of it on alcohol and women while abandoning his many children and wife at home, leaving them without food to eat or warm clothes to wear. There was never enough to go around in the big family—especially love.

Sometime before Domingo was seven, his parents separated and his mother moved the family to California. She lied to property owners about how many children she had in order to rent a home in North Hollywood. No one would have rented to her had they known there would be one parent and ten children living in the two-bedroom house.

His dad was in and out of the house even after the separation, bringing violence and wreaking havoc when he did. Once when Domingo's sister played an Elvis record, their father put his fist through the brand-new stereo she had bought after saving for a long time. Another time he backhanded Domingo's disabled sister, then hit Domingo's mom when she tried to intervene—and when Domingo's brothers stood up for their mom, their dad would get mad. Before long, everyone was either bleeding or crying. Then their dad would just leave and not come back for months at a time.

Domingo walked to school with his older and younger sisters—some of the time without shoes. He struggled to read because he hadn't learned the fundamentals; they moved so often, he couldn't catch up. Occasionally, kind people noticed this little boy in need. One of his special memories is of an elementary school teacher who took him to the store after school to buy a pair of shoes.

One of Domingo's biggest disappointments was that he wanted to play baseball ... but didn't know how. He'd sit for hours on the curbs of his neighborhood watching the other boys play pickup games of street baseball. His own brothers were off working or drinking somewhere. So day after day, hour after hour, he'd just sit and watch. He didn't have a ball, a glove, or a bat. He didn't know how to use any of those things anyway. His father never taught him. Never threw one ball for him to catch. He couldn't play in a league because his family didn't have the money. He would have been happy to just play ball in the street, but none of the kids ever invited him to play.

His hours on the curb gave him a lot of time to think. *Is there a reason they get to play and I don't? Why is this? Are they better than me?* He couldn't help but notice his exclusion from other worlds—ones where kids went to Disneyland and baseball games, ate out with their intact families, and took family vacations.

One day, as he sat on the curb in the California sunshine, he thought about the God he'd heard of while growing up in Baptist churches—and he wondered where this God was. Why was Domingo always hungry, and why did his mom have to suffer so much?

His life was not anything like those of the kids who played ball in the street. He came to the conclusion that if there was a God, he was obviously unjust and unfair and Domingo wanted nothing to do with him. He was a good kid until that point. But sitting on those curbs, thinking a lot about God, changed him. He rejected God and went his own way.

At age eleven, he began cutting school and getting into fights. He'd go to the local liquor store and steal pints of whiskey and packs of cigarettes. The clerks never suspected that this sweet little kid with his nose in a magazine was stealing from them. Domingo stashed his goods in the drawers in his bedroom. In the middle of the night, some-one would knock on his window and say, "Hey, Domingo. Whatcha got?" And Domingo would open the window and his dresser drawers to display what he had in his "store." Money and goods exchanged hands. And the more money he had, the more he wanted to make. He saw what money could do for him. He liked treating his family to ice cream, as well as the other comforts money gave them.

At twelve, he'd been drinking beer for nearly a year while hang-ing out with his older brothers and cousins. One night when the *familia* went to Jack in the Box for a burger, their rivals from San Fernando showed up. In the subsequent fight, one of Domingo's cousins got knifed. Twelve-year-old Domingo, who had never driven a car, jumped into the driver's seat, the other boys dove in, and he drove them to safety.

The police started getting involved. They'd take Domingo home and deposit him at the front door. Minutes later he was out the back door, off to do the same things that had gotten him into trouble in the first place. But then, finally, his revolving door shut.

A judge sent him to juvenile hall—not for anything specific, but after so many small offenses, the judge felt that Domingo, who had no authority figure or supervision, was headed down the wrong path. The judge hoped juvenile hall would help get him back on the right one. Domingo was able to get out four months later when his sister and brother-in-law took him into their home. Although he was only thirteen, they required him to buy groceries and pay rent. He earned the money by working for his brother-in-law at his automotive shop.

There was really nothing good about Domingo's childhood. This little boy never got to play. He never knew if his needs would be met. He knew his mother loved him, and she did what she could with what she had—but she didn't have much either. By the time he was thirteen, he was a beaten-down alcoholic with a rap sheet, time spent in juvenile hall, and no parents, and he was working like an adult to pay rent and buy groceries. His role models were alcoholics, womanizers, rebellious teens, and guys who dealt with their anger by beating on someone.

This kid didn't have a chance.

meeting Domingo

My friend and I were giggling and talking as we walked around the Northridge Junior High School campus. It was a new school year, and we were both excited about being in junior high for the first time. As we rounded a corner so I could take a drink from the fountain, I saw the new Mexican boy everyone was talking about. I couldn't believe it—he was smoking a cigarette on campus! I thought he was so fearless and good-looking. Then, with all the sureness in the world, I turned to my friend and announced, "I'm going to marry him."

My friend just rolled her eyes. I watched him laughing and goofing around with the other guys. Sure, he was cute, but there was something more. He was cocky. Confident.

When we were introduced, he didn't say much—in fact, he ignored me. Then later he asked if I wanted to meet him at the skating rink. I was so excited, but I had to babysit. When I got to the skating rink late, I found him making out with my friend. I knew right away I was in over my head, but for whatever reason, I continued to like him and wanted him to notice me.

I was so surprised the first time Domingo called. As my heart pounded, we had some sort of simple conversation. It didn't matter what we said. I was hooked. He started calling me frequently, and we hung out together in school. One time when he walked me home from school, we saw my mom. We ducked into the bushes, afraid and laughing at the same time. And then he kissed me. My first real kiss. I thought it was wonderful, and from that moment, Domingo had my heart. I wanted to spend as much time with him as I could. I thought it was true love. But when my father, who was so strict he wouldn't allow me to talk to boys, found out I liked Domingo, he told me I couldn't date or have him over until I was fifteen. But his command didn't stop me from seeing Domingo at school and the skating rink.

When my fifteenth birthday came close, I could hardly wait. Domingo and I could stop sneaking around! But when I turned fifteen, my dad said he had changed his mind. I fought and argued with him. I yelled at him. And then I shrieked, "I hate you!" and ran to my room, slammed the door, and cried. I was crying because I couldn't have Domingo over. But I was also devastated because my dad, my hero, had lied to me.

What I didn't understand was that my dad knew what kind of boy Domingo was—he reminded my father of himself at that age. Like most young teen girls, I had blinders on. I could see Domingo only as the boy of my dreams, while my father was trying to do his job as a father and protect me.

My father began to keep a close eye on me. That meant that, in order to see Domingo, I had to lie about everything. It meant cutting school and going to Domingo's house. It meant my sister Billie taking us with her when she went places. It meant telling my mom I was babysitting when, in reality, the only person I was "babysitting" was Domingo. To make the whole thing believable, Domingo gave me the money I would have earned had I really babysat. I didn't care that I had become so deceitful. Domingo had become my whole world. He was popular in school, I was his girlfriend, and nothing else mattered.

A determined spirit is one of Domingo's strongest character qualities. How he did all he did, I will never know. He was such a hard worker. At fifteen he went to school until noon, then worked at his brother-in-law's auto shop until after midnight—and he was great at it. He could work on any engine and understood them so well he could modify them to make them better and faster. After work he sometimes hung around with the guys and drank beer, then went home. Several nights a week he'd walk the two and a half miles to my house and rap on my window. I'd let him in, and we'd whisper quietly in my room until my father got home around two. Then Domingo would slip out through the window and walk home.

When we were alone, in the dark of our whispers, Domingo shared his past with me and the heartaches he had endured while growing up in a very difficult environment. It was then I discovered he'd had to be a fighter in order to survive. Throughout his childhood he had learned a lot of things no boy should have to learn, and as a result, he'd made promises to himself that affected his future in positive and negative ways.

But with too much time alone in the dark, two teenagers at the peak of their raging hormones find other things to do besides talk. I was stupid and naive, and not surprisingly, I lost my innocence.

When a girl meets a boy she likes, and she's old enough, it's supposed to be fun going on dates and doing things together. But during my time with Domingo there were no fun events or happy dates—just worries about getting caught.

One time Domingo and I had fallen asleep fully clothed on top of my bed when my dad came home and opened my door. I will never forget the sound of the door opening or his face when he saw me with Domingo. Shock. Disappointment. He didn't yell or get angry; he just quietly handled the situation. He called the police while I sat, quietly crying in the living room, terrified. Domingo sat in the kitchen with his head down, his hands dangling between his legs as he waited for my dad to blow.

The police came and questioned Domingo and looked up his record. I had no idea he had such a long rap sheet. I knew some of the stuff because he'd told me. But there were surprises on that list even for me. I didn't like what I heard. I'd admired this boy who did so much with so little. His tenacious and creative character that never gave up. No matter what the obstacles, he figured out a way to work through or around them and thrive, not just survive. I loved his kind and giving heart. I loved talking to him and hearing what he thought about things. He was affectionate and seemed happy to care for me.

But I had begun to see a different side of him. He wasn't always fun and happy—he had a dark and scary side, one that was controlling and angry and very jealous. We had started to fight all the time. I wasn't so sure I liked him or trusted him to be good to me. That night I realized my dad was right and I was wrong. I decided to break up with Domingo and begin mending my relationship with my dad.

chapter 2

fear and marriage

One day when I was at a friend's house, her sister commented that I was starting to fill out. It felt like the world froze. Everyone was looking at me. "You look like you're pregnant," she said.

"Don't talk to me like that in front of everybody," I said, fuming. "It's not right." I stomped out of the house. After calming down a little, I tried to remember when my last cycle had been. Since I was irregular, missing one period was not unusual. But a cold chill crept up my back as I tried to think. Fear crawled in and replaced my anger. *What if I really am pregnant?*

I was scared but didn't know what to do, so I kept it to myself. Within a few weeks I knew for sure I was pregnant. At breakfast I would get up from the table to go throw up.

A friend who worked for a doctor's office told me that when I turned sixteen in a couple of weeks I'd be old enough to come in by myself to see if I was pregnant. (There were no home pregnancy tests back then.) I was never afraid of being a mother, but I was afraid of hurting my family, so I started to look for homes for unwed mothers and began saving my money to run away. What I knew for certain was that I didn't want any part of Domingo anymore.

So after my sixteenth birthday in June, I went to the doctor to find out what I already knew was the truth. When the doctor told me I was three months along, I was numb. I knew this would shame my whole family, and I wanted to die. But I also knew I had to tell Domingo. It wasn't what I wanted, but I knew it was the right thing to do. My friend who worked for the doctor had already alerted Domingo to the possibility, and he had been angry that I hadn't told him. But what would he do when he knew for sure? How would he react?

As I drove into the auto-shop parking lot, I took a deep breath. I turned to unlock the door, but my hands were shaking so badly that it took me a moment to be able to pull up the button. I stepped out of the car and tried to gather all my strength. I could hear the whoosh of the air compressor, the clank of tools, the shouts of guys as they bantered back and forth over their work. The strong smell of engine oil, brake fluid, and gas mixed with my fear and made it hard for me to keep my breakfast down. I took in another deep breath, but it didn't help. I knew all the rosaries wouldn't save me from what I'd done. What *we'd* done. I bowed my head. I refused to cry. I had too much pride for tears. I'd show everybody, including Domingo, that I had it all under control.

"Hey, Irene."

I popped my head up. Domingo's brother-in-law who owned the shop stood there, wiping his hands on a blue shop towel. "Mingo's in the clean room, building an engine."

I tried to smile at him, but feeling the shame rise inside me, I quickly turned my head instead. My knees softened and felt as though they wouldn't hold me up much longer. I looked away and walked through the shop, hoping not to have any eye contact with the guys who were working. I wondered what Domingo had shared with them. What did they know? What did they think about me? My face flamed, and the words I imagined stuck in my belly. Words that made me hate myself. Made me sick. Who was I trying to fool? I wasn't strong. I didn't have a plan. I had thought at sixteen I was so mature and knew so much. Really, I was just a lost and confused child.

I stepped into the clean room. "Domingo," I said to his back. He turned to face me.

"Hey, Irene. What's up?"

"I'm pregnant." Humiliation washed over me as I said the words.

Domingo froze. He stared off into space, saying nothing.

I looked down at my black shoes, waiting, bracing myself for the ugly words I knew would come.

"There's only one thing to do," Domingo said in his strong, confident voice. "Get married as soon as possible. I will take care of you. You and the baby. You don't have to worry about anything."

I was relieved that he accepted I was carrying his child. Then, with a sense of pride, I wondered at this sixteen-year-old boy acting like a grown man. How confident he was. That he promised to take care of us. He put many grown men to shame with his stance.

Then panic seeped in. My heart felt heavy and fearful. A wave of conflicting emotions piled in on top of the others. I didn't really want to marry him. I didn't even like him, not anymore. He wasn't who I had thought he was.

Even so, I felt trapped. Where else could I go? What other options did I have? If I didn't marry Domingo, my life was doomed.

What man would want to take me as his wife after I had committed such a despicable act? There was really nothing I could do but agree with him.

getting permission

Domingo took me home and waited outside for my dad to get home from work. When Dad arrived, he was in a good mood, and I hated knowing I was going to destroy that mood. "Dad," I said, trembling, "I have to talk to you."

"What's wrong, Rene?" He looked concerned.

"I have committed the worst act a young girl can do." I swallowed, then took a deep breath. "I'm pregnant."

Shock and disbelief took the place where concern had been.

"Domingo's outside, waiting to talk to you."

At that, my father erupted. "Tell that boy I don't want to see him or talk to him." I walked out of the room to tell Domingo he needed to leave.

"I want to talk to your father," he said, his anger climbing to the level of my father's.

"No, Mingo. Please. Please go now."

Domingo spun on his heels and stormed away to his car.

Telling my mother was no easier. She kept saying, "What did I do to deserve this?"

I wanted to die because I had disgraced her. My parents were cold and distant to me that night. I felt like they were looking at me with disgust and anger. So I retreated to my room and cried myself to sleep.

The next morning, Domingo showed up on the doorstep. He didn't even wait to be invited in but moved past me toward my father's bedroom. Then in a strong and defiant voice Domingo said, "I want to talk to your father."

"No! He doesn't want to speak with you."

"I don't care." Domingo's fist pounded on the bedroom door. "I want to talk to you, Manuel. I'm not leaving until we talk." Again, he didn't wait to be invited; he stormed in and closed the door behind him.

I paced outside, listening to angry voices rise and fall. Finally, Domingo emerged. He looked me in the eye and said, "We're getting married." And then he left.

I couldn't believe my father had given his permission. He later told me he knew Domingo was a good boy because he fought hard to do the honorable thing, even after my father told him he didn't have to marry me. Dad told him he would care for me and the baby, but Domingo wouldn't hear of it. It was his baby, and he was going to marry me no matter what.

Once my dad said we could get married, I felt a sense of excitement, urgency, and panic. Because we both had just turned sixteen, we had to get permission from a doctor, a priest, our parents, and a judge. The doctor tried talking us out of getting married, and the priest told us to give the baby up for adoption or consider other options available to us. We were stunned. I couldn't believe our priest was telling us to consider an illegal abortion.

No one wanted us to get married. Everyone around Domingo encouraged him not to do it. The guys at the shop told Domingo it wasn't his responsibility. Even most of the counselors at our school told Domingo, "Don't get married. You have too much of life ahead of you."

The one person who went to bat for him was Mr. Ferguson, our high school counselor. Because Domingo scored so high on his mechanical aptitude test, Mr. Ferguson felt Domingo's job at the auto shop was the right fit. He got permission for Domingo to attend night school as a minor so he could continue to work weekdays and go to Saturday continuation school to earn his diploma. Mr. Ferguson was the only person who didn't criticize; rather, he did all he could to help. Without him, we couldn't have done it.

I wasn't paying as much attention to the negative things people were saying. All I could think of was getting this list of things done so I could get married. Then everything would be okay. My sin would be washed away.

Our last permissions hurdle was getting the judge's approval. We arrived at the courthouse early in the morning. My father had come on my behalf, and Domingo's mother had come on his. We were all sent to the courtroom and were told the judge would see us during his recess from presiding over divorce court. We sat there in silence, watching all the broken marriages parade by, one couple after another pleading their cases before the judge. It was ugly to see so many couples wanting a divorce. When had their love turned into such hatred?

Fear played in my belly, pulling my thoughts in many directions at once. I wasn't afraid of getting married, but I was afraid of Domingo.

After at least four hours of waiting, the judge finally summoned us into his chambers. We stood before his massive desk. He looked at our parents and said, "How do you feel about these kids getting married?"

My future mother-in-law looked grim. "It's the right thing to do."

"I think they should wait and not get married," my father said.

The judge addressed Domingo. "How do you feel about all this?"

"I'm ready," he said proudly. "I've rented a room for us, I have a job, and I'm finishing school on Saturdays."

The judge looked us both over and said, "I'm not going to give permission for you to marry. Come back when you're eighteen." He closed the open file folder, his body language dismissing us.

A bomb went off inside of me. It had never occurred to me that he would say no! *Oh, dear God, what will I do now?*

Next to me, Domingo fumed. I could tell by the look on his face that he was going to blow up. I felt I was going to be sick. I knew Domingo was determined, strong willed, and defiant. No one was going to tell him what he could or couldn't do. He might be only sixteen, but he'd been on his own since he was eleven.

"What are you thinking?" the judge asked him, probably seeing the rage in Domingo's eyes.

Domingo stood up and said, "I don't care what any of you think or say. It's my child, and I'm going to take care of it, and no one can keep me from that. I will figure out some way and will run away if I have to, but I will marry Irene."

Once again, I was amazed at the strength and courage of this young boy. First to stand up to my father and then to the judge. I wanted to feel happy and protected. But I knew better. Still, there was hope in my heart that he would be different when we were married.

The judge gave a small, smug smile and said, "All right. You can get married." That was it! He had been testing Domingo, and Domingo had passed with flying colors. Many years later my dad shared that the judge had come to him and said, "I don't know why, but I feel they will never get a divorce. They will stay married forever."

wedding day

My clock radio went off, startling me awake after I'd barely dozed off. The night had been long as I struggled to get to sleep. I rolled over and turned off the alarm. My dad had given the clock radio to me for my sixteenth birthday. We were both excited as I opened it—he because he had picked it out himself, and me because it was from my dad and we'd finally made peace after a long year of anger and frustration. And it was the only birthday gift I could remember ever receiving. But that didn't matter because it was so special to get this wonderful gift from my father.

Today was the last day I would wake up in my room. Tomorrow I'd wake up in another home, one I didn't know very well. At least the radio was mine and I could take it with me to my new home.

This was not at all how I dreamed my wedding day would be. I had imagined myself in a white dress, walking down the aisle of the Catholic church. There had even been a time when I dreamed it would be Domingo waiting for me at the altar, wearing a black tuxedo.

The previous night, Domingo had asked my father if he could take me out on a date. Even though Domingo and I had spent many hours together, we'd never gone on a real date. With my dad's permission, we went to a movie and got a burger. For a few hours, I could imagine I was a normal girl experiencing a normal date. I was so young. And I was a dreamer, so good at pretending.

As we sat across the table from each other, I asked, "Domingo, are you afraid of getting married?"

He gave me a small smile. "I have been alone for so long. I'm looking forward to taking care of you and our baby."

That was the first time in a long time I felt hope. Maybe I had judged him wrongly. Maybe he did love me after all.

I threw the light covers back, got out of bed, and took my pink lace dress out of my closet. It wasn't anything special, but it was my best dress. Domingo had mentioned he liked it, so I felt it would work for the occasion.

There was no excitement surrounding the day. My mom never asked me if I needed money or if I had something special to wear. Really, no one asked. No one seemed to care. My family had planned no celebration. This was supposed to be the happiest day of my life. Instead, I was filled with fear, sadness, and shame. What would happen now? What kind of husband would Domingo be? We were only sixteen and didn't know as much as we thought we did.

I went into the bedroom where my mother was still sleeping. I gently shook her shoulder, then stood back. "Mom," I whispered. "Mom."

She opened her eyes and gave me a cold stare. She barely moved. And she didn't say a word.

"Are you going to come to see me get married?"

"No, Rene," she said. "I'm too tired. I'll see you when you come back." And then she rolled over and said nothing more.

I waited, hoping she would speak again, tell me she loved me, or at least wish me luck. But there was nothing. I turned and walked out of the room, hating myself for what I had done. I'd brought so much pain and embarrassment to my mom and family. No one wanted to be a part of me anymore. No one could bear to see me get married. There was no one but me, and I had to be strong for my baby.

I straightened with determination. I would show everyone they were wrong about us. Domingo had a plan, and maybe if I was good, it would work. It wasn't much, but it was something I could hold on to.

After my shower, I attempted to eat, but the knots in my stomach wouldn't allow it. I zipped my dress, curled my hair, and put on my makeup. No matter what our circumstances, I wanted Domingo to be pleased when he saw me. As I went to the full-length mirror to see how I looked, I touched my belly. The life inside me was more apparent than I wanted it to be. This was a day I wanted to conceal my pregnancy, not reveal it. But what else could I do?

A noise in the kitchen lifted my heart. I thought my mom had changed her mind. I slipped on my shoes and went to see her. Instead, it was my sister Billie who was getting ready to go with us. Although I was sad my mom hadn't changed her mind, I was relieved and thankful Billie was coming.

"Of course I'm coming," she told me. "I wouldn't miss the day my sister is getting married." She looked me over and smiled. "You look beautiful." And then she hugged me. Oh, how I loved her.

Domingo arrived in his newly painted 1957 Chevy. We could hear the engine rumble as he parked it in the driveway. He came through the front door, looking incredibly handsome in a black suit.

He glanced at me and gave me a sweet smile. In the same breath he asked me if I was ready to get married and told me I looked nice. As odd as it seemed, his words gave me a sense of connection. My heart was softening, and the fear inside seemed to be slowly slipping away.

As we drove through the canyon to get to the Malibu courthouse, I was in deep thought. I would be a good wife, cooking, cleaning, and working hard to please my husband.

When we got to the courthouse, the clerk waved us to the justice of the peace's office. Domingo, Billie, the witnesses, and I stood in line with many other couples, most quiet and not looking around. I kept my eyes down, shuffling forward each time the door opened and closed. I felt like we were on an assembly line.

Domingo grabbed my hand in such an intimate and possessive way that it startled me. *It's going to be okay*, I thought, trying to reassure myself. At one point, Billie grabbed my other hand and squeezed it, giving me a slight smile. I was so glad she was there with me.

As I walked into the chambers, I looked around and thought again how this was the day I had dreamed of since I was a little girl— but it was so far from what I had imagined. There was no music, no long aisle, no rice throwing, just a quick "I do." And it was done.

On our way back to the car, a comforting thought rolled through me. I was now a married woman. I no longer had to feel ashamed of the life that was growing inside me. Our present-day society doesn't understand how different it was back then. Staying pure until you were married was something to be proud of; being unmarried and pregnant brought great shame. Many young girls were sent away when they got pregnant in order to hide that shame. I was lucky. I was with a boy who wanted to marry me and care for his child.

We took our time driving back through Malibu Canyon, getting ice cream along the way. Domingo was in a good mood—something I never expected. He reached over and took my hand again, telling me he was excited about our new life. I didn't answer because I was so confused. I didn't know how I felt.

As Domingo turned into the driveway of my house, I thought of how I had left that morning as a girl but was returning a woman. I was now Mrs. Domingo Garcia. I felt a sense of peace and gratification as I thought of my new name.

My dad had gone to work, but my mom was sitting outside with my aunt. I apologized to them for being later than we had planned. Mom looked at me and replied, "I'm no longer responsible for you, *hija*; you're a married woman now."

It was so matter-of-fact. Almost like a changing of the guard. I tried not to let my disappointment show. "I'm going to get my things."

She shrugged and waved her hand dismissively.

Domingo followed me inside to carry out a box that held my few clothes. After he left, I unplugged my clock radio and wound the cord gently around it. I looked around the room, thinking how it would never be mine again. "Good-bye," I whispered as I closed the door.

Since Domingo was still living with his sister and brother-in-law, the small room he rented from them would now be ours. After we put my few things away, we changed our clothes and went to a party already in full swing at the neighbors' house. I felt uncomfortable and out of place. Not much of a honeymoon.

When we returned to our little room that night, I really wanted to go home. I missed Billie. I had moved to live with people I didn't know, in a house I wasn't familiar with, and with a husband I didn't love. I was terrified. It was as though I was living someone else's life. I crawled into bed and faced the wall so Domingo wouldn't see the tears streaming down my face. I hoped I had paid the penance for my sin and would be forgiven.

Domingo put his arm over me and said good night. It gave me an odd sense of security, and I wondered why he was not afraid. In fact, he had seemed happy the whole day.

the first days

The next morning we arranged our room and talked about his schedule for the following day, when he would need to get up at 4:00 a.m. We talked about my responsibilities and what I would do. He told me this was somebody else's house, so I needed to be respectful and cautious.

After I made our bed, I went to see how I could help my new sister-in-law. I was excited she had invited the family over for a party to celebrate our marriage. I felt as though they accepted me and wanted to get to know me.

Later that afternoon Domingo's family began to arrive. They seemed very welcoming. I didn't know until much later that his family members had made bets on how long we would be married.

I was engaged in conversation with my sister-in-law when the doorbell rang. In swaggered some guys from Domingo's work, slapping him on the back and saying crude things about his new status. Domingo's demeanor changed from happy and at ease to dark and withdrawn. He'd been drinking ever since the beer had been set out in coolers filled with ice, and since drinking could change his mood so quickly, I thought maybe that was why he didn't seem happy to see the guys from work. The doorbell continued to ring, and unfamiliar people continued to stream in. I smiled and greeted everyone politely but felt a little overwhelmed.

Domingo whispered in my ear to follow him to the bedroom. I sensed a difference in his tone, but I wasn't sure what was wrong. "Mingo, what is it?" I asked when we got inside the room.

"Irene, you need to stay in here and not come out for the rest of the night," he said.

"What? What's wrong? Why? I can't stay in the room. This party is for me, too." I couldn't think of anything more rude and disrespectful. "I can't stay here," I said in a strong and defiant tone. "I'm going out there."

I didn't see it coming. I only felt a sudden, powerful pain on the side of my face where his fist landed. Without another word, he walked out and shut the door behind him. I dropped onto the bed and sobbed, cradling my throbbing cheek.

As I lay on the bed, I ran through my few options. Mom would say I deserved what I got. Dad wouldn't help me. Billie couldn't. I would just have to endure this alone. I got angry at myself for letting fear dictate my inaction. Fear that Domingo would hit me again. Fear that everyone would hear us fighting. Fear that people would see what Domingo was really like. Despite everything, I wanted people to see the best in him. And I guess I felt I was a reflection of him. In a weird way I thought being silent was a way to protect my reputation as well.

I finally surrendered to Domingo's will and got into bed, excluded from my own party. I tried to get to sleep in the midst of the sounds of our celebration. Laughter, music, and shouts just out of reach were another sign that my marriage was not starting out even remotely as I had imagined.

The next morning Domingo, no longer stern or angry, held me and told me in his soft, tender voice that he had wanted and expected to have only his family there. He wanted our party to be special and private. Instead, his sister and brother-in-law invited people he didn't like and people he didn't know, turning our celebration into an excuse for them to throw a party for themselves. He wanted to protect me from the guys he did know. In his anger and frustration, he had lashed out at me.

"I'm sorry I hurt you, Irene. I want to be married and have my own family. I want it to be just us."

The first few months we were married were difficult for both of us, even as life settled into a routine. Domingo got up and went to work every day, leaving at 5:00 a.m. At 5:00 p.m., the racers would start coming to the shop with six-packs of beer, ready to check out the engines that were being built. They would all drink, and sometimes Domingo would work until early morning. I don't think anyone realized how old Domingo was—either that, or they didn't care that they were providing alcohol to a minor.

When Domingo wasn't drinking, life was reasonably okay. But on the nights when he stayed at the shop and drank, he would come home late and in a foul mood. He would start in on me, saying awful things, often lashing out physically. My only defense was my words, and I used them to strike back. Oh, how I hated him then. I wanted out of our marriage, but good girls didn't get divorced—especially pregnant ones.

Even sober, Domingo wanted to control everything I did. And he did a good job.

One morning my father came to the door and asked me to go to breakfast with him. "I have to ask Domingo first," I told him, excited he had come for me.

"Of course, that's fine."

I called Domingo at work and told him my dad was there and asked him if I could go out to breakfast.

"No," Domingo said, and that was it. No explanation. Nothing.

Shocked, I wanted to understand why he said no, but I didn't dare ask. As I hung up, I knew I had two choices: to go with my dad and deal with the consequences or to please Domingo and hurt my dad. I was ashamed that once again I let fear dictate my decision. Embarrassed, I went to tell my father. "I'm sorry, Dad. Domingo said I can't go."

"That's okay, Rene. You do what your husband tells you to." He turned and walked away, leaving me to feel incredibly sad that I couldn't spend time with my own father.

I really didn't know if marriage was supposed to be like that because no one except Domingo had ever told me what my role as a wife should be. My dad was easygoing and let my mom do pretty much whatever she wanted. Domingo's dad had been possessive and didn't let his mom do anything or go anywhere. Her job had been to stay home.

I soon learned what was expected of me. I was to clean my sister-in-law's house every morning, then go to my room for the rest of the day. In the evening I cooked dinner. I loved cooking because it brought me great satisfaction, and it felt good when Domingo praised it in front of everyone.

Domingo worked hard. Even though he often didn't get home until 10:00 p.m. or later, he never complained. This boy had so much stamina, and he liked providing for his new family. The automotive shop where he worked was a good, clean shop with a great reputation.

We were so very different from each other. I'd had a strict upbringing, and he'd done whatever he wanted. I was naive; he was street-smart. I was a dreamer; he was a planner. The differences between us didn't matter to me. I was determined to make my marriage work no matter what. I would prove to everyone who had laughed at us that we would never get a divorce. That would be tough for two sixteen-year-old kids each doing what they felt was right in their own eyes, considering themselves more important than the other.

There was much about Domingo I didn't know. At night he sometimes shared stories about growing up. As a result of his childhood of neglect, he promised me he would never let his child go without food, clothing, and shelter. These stories chiseled the hardness of my heart away.

I looked forward to him coming home on the nights he didn't drink, when it seemed like I was the most important person in the world to him. During these times, my heart would draw close to him, and I thought things would be okay. And some weekends were wonderful—those when we went to visit his family or mine. My mother loved my husband and not only treated him as special but kissed and hugged him as his face grew bright red. But on other weekends, reality would yank me back to the place of anguish and pain. To the boy I didn't understand and was afraid of. The problem was, he was never able to have just one drink, so when he drank, he got drunk. Many times we got through the night without incident. But if I did something wrong or said something he didn't like, there would be consequences.

Domingo always apologized the following morning. He was sorry and promised it would never happen again. But I didn't let it go or forgive him. Instead, I used my words like weapons. I wanted to wound him. I wanted him to feel the pain I had felt the night before. I'm not excusing his behavior, but I was not completely innocent either.

And I did pray that things would change. I begged God to make Domingo the nice boy I knew he could be when he wasn't drinking.

But the truth was, I hated my husband. Hated him.

chapter 3

becoming a family

Shortly before the baby was due, my mom and sister-in-law threw me a surprise baby shower. When I entered my parents' house and scanned the living room, it seemed as though everyone I had ever known was there. I broke down and cried. Were they all really there to support me? I had a hard time thinking that could be true. But there they were, all happy faces looking at me. Beyond them was a wall lined to the top with presents. I had never seen so many presents in one place before. I felt a joyful peace knowing our baby would have everything it would need.

The shower was kind of a coming-out party for me. All these people acknowledging I was a married woman. Up until then I was so embarrassed about being pregnant. But now I felt accepted. Everyone was so kind to me. Even my mom was no longer upset with me. She had forgiven me, she loved my husband, and I knew she would love my baby. She was clearly excited to be a grandmother. And the thing that most surprised me was my mother's obvious pride in me.

From that point on, my relationship with my mother starting growing into something stronger and better than we'd ever had. But I never could tell her what was really going on in my marriage. I was determined I would never embarrass her again.

kicked

One Saturday evening, not long before the baby was due, Domingo and I got into another fight. I didn't want him to go out with a friend he always seemed to get into trouble with. I knew they would most likely be drinking and maybe hanging out with girls. Only two weeks earlier I had walked into a kitchen at a party and saw Domingo making out with another girl.

"Why are you going, Mingo? You know I don't want you to go."

He stood in the hall bathroom, fixing his hair. He said nothing, ignoring me—which infuriated me.

"Where are you going?" I demanded. He still wouldn't answer me. I grabbed his upper arm to get him to pay attention to me. "Why can't you stay home? Please stay home with me."

Our relationship had become so caustic that it took only a split second before the anger in both of us erupted into rage-filled behavior—me with my mouth, Domingo with his strength. As he swung his arm to get me away from him, I could see the look of disgust in his eyes. I lost my balance and fell to the floor. I cried, wrenching on the ground as sobs and spasms swept over me. My body blocked his way out of the bathroom. Just before he stepped over me, he kicked me in the stomach. I don't think he intended to hurt me. He was just so disgusted and frustrated with me.

My sobs grew stronger, not because I was hurt, but because I felt like a piece of garbage, ugly and used, someone my husband didn't want to be with. I just wanted to be loved. I felt he kicked me the way he would have kicked a piece of furniture he'd stubbed his toe against.

By Monday, when the baby still hadn't moved, I knew I had to go to the doctor. I was nervous, not knowing what to tell him. The doctor looked at me, his eyes narrowing. "Did anything happen?"

"I fell," I said. I figured it was sort of true. I *had* fallen.

The doctor put on his stethoscope and moved it around my belly. "Yes, there's a heartbeat," he said, and all the tension and worry slipped out of me.

"Sometimes the baby will get quiet and not move as much." He set the stethoscope on the counter. "Everything is fine. But I want you to be careful."

The way he said it made me think the doctor knew the truth. My marriage was not good.

birth

"Are you coming or not?" Domingo asked, grabbing the car keys off the counter and opening the door that led to the dark winter's night.

"Yes, Mingo." I sighed. "I'm coming." I didn't really want to go, but I didn't want to stay home either. I didn't feel well, but I couldn't really describe what it was. Besides, we were only going to the house of some friends, where we'd hang out with the usual crowd.

When we got to the house, I put my donation of guacamole and tortilla chips on the kitchen table. Domingo eyed me carefully. "What's wrong?"

"I don't know. I don't feel good." The baby wasn't due for a few weeks, and I was told the first baby is always late, so I just thought I was getting sick. Throughout the evening I continued to squirm—too uncomfortable to sit still and too achy to stand.

Again he asked. Then again. I could tell he was getting frustrated with me for not telling him what was wrong. He didn't say he was worried about me.

Despite how badly I felt, we stayed late, then went back to our room and crawled into bed.

In the middle of the night, something warm and wet woke me. I thought my water had broken, but when I turned on the light, all I saw was blood everywhere. When I got out of bed, I kept bleeding. Domingo called the doctor, who told him to bring me in immediately.

At the hospital they didn't waste any time finding me a room. Domingo sat there with me, trying to encourage me. He held my hand even though I squeezed so tightly during the contractions that I left marks on his hand. He never complained, and I could tell he felt bad for me when the pains came. I wanted to scream because it hurt so badly, but I was too embarrassed. I hadn't taken any birthing classes, and no one had taught me how to breathe or what to do to make it through the increasingly painful and difficult contractions.

Whenever the doctor came to examine me, he sent Domingo out of the room. The nurses encouraged Domingo to go home. "It's going to be a long time before the baby comes, so you might as well go home and get some rest." I wasn't happy that they told him to leave, but we thought we needed to do what we were told, so Domingo reluctantly left.

Between contractions, as I lay in the labor room alone, I thought about my life. There was so much uncertainty about how life would change with a child in my arms. Would Domingo still drink and hurt me? Would he love our baby? Oh, I hoped he'd change. Maybe a child would give him the desire to stop drinking.

Another strong contraction left me breathless.

I prayed God would intervene in our marriage. "Please, God. Change my life and help me be a good mom."

Voices in the hallway broke off my prayer. "Two babies having a baby," I heard my nurse say.

Funny, I didn't feel like a baby. I felt like a grown woman.

A few hours later, Domingo was back, and I was really glad to see him. Not long after, he was sent home again. Domingo left, but he assured me he would return.

After eighteen hours of hard labor—bleeding the entire time—I was exhausted and scared. But I thought my labor was hard because I had sinned and gotten pregnant. I wondered if God would ever forgive me. I had told no one about the guilt that sat so heavily in my heart.

Again I heard voices whispering in the hallway about me, pieces of words that didn't make sense—but clearly something wasn't right. Was I going to make it? Was the baby?

I didn't want to be alone. I was in so much pain, and I wanted Domingo there. I knew he would tell me it would all be okay. Now I wondered if he would go out with his friends or if he would show up for the birth of his baby. I wanted him to be next to me. I needed to be loved and held, but I was so alone.

As another powerful contraction took hold of my body, Domingo came into the room, the nurse trailing behind him.

"Why don't you do something to help her?" Domingo demanded.

"We'd like to," the nurse said. "But she's hemorrhaging so much that the doctor doesn't want to risk doing a C-section."

I was so exhausted, I had nothing left in me. After a few more contractions the doctor came in, examined me, and said, "If you don't stop bleeding soon, we'll be forced to take the baby any way we can."

I suppose I should have been scared. Instead, I rolled to my side obediently when the nurse came in to give me an epidural. Then she popped up the metal railings on either side of the bed and began to push me toward delivery. Domingo was told to wait outside.

There was a flurry of activity as they set me up on the bed and covered me with a sheet. The doctor rolled a stool to the foot of the bed and sat on it. After a few contractions the doctor began yelling at the nurses because the baby wasn't coming out.

I was so naive that I didn't understand all that was going on around me. I didn't know how serious the situation was. Nor did I really care at this point. I don't remember how long this went on, nor what the exact problem was that kept the baby from being delivered. I was numb and felt no pain. I was so out of it that it all felt like a dream.

Then someone called out, "It's a boy!"

I moved to look at him and will never forget the feeling that completely flooded me when I saw my boy. "He's so tiny," I managed to say.

At the same moment, the doctor and nurse said, "Tiny? He's a *big* boy."

After wiping him down, they wrapped him in a blanket and laid him next to me, where I could feel his warmth. Oh, I fell completely in love with this little baby. It was then that I understood the beauty of giving birth. It's the hardest pain a woman will bear, and yet the minute she sees her child it's all forgotten. In that moment nothing mattered but the instinct of wanting to hold and protect that tiny creature. It was the most amazing feeling in my life.

As they wheeled me out of delivery, Domingo was standing there, waiting, as proud as could be. I said, "Look at him, Domingo. He's so beautiful."

Domingo had a funny look on his face. Only later did I learn that he didn't think our boy was beautiful. The doctor had used forceps to deliver him, so his head wasn't shaped quite right. Domingo was worried there was something wrong with him. And yet he too fell in love with his boy the moment he saw him. It seemed like he glowed as he tenderly touched our boy's face. I don't know why, but at that moment I felt a sense of peace for my boy—but deep heartache for me.

after the baby

A week after Anthony was born, we were able to get our first apartment. We had to lie and say we were eighteen to get the landlord to rent to us. It was a small one-bedroom, but it was ours.

I earned extra money by babysitting and doing other odd jobs while Domingo worked all day—except for Tuesdays and Thursdays when he went to night school at the junior college. He'd drop me and Anthony off at my mom's on the way to school and pick us up on the way back. Once we got home, I did his English and science homework, he did the math, and we shared history.

Most afternoons Domingo was able to come home for lunch, so as a good little wife I was happy to make it for him. It was enjoyable to be together then, the little married couple as new parents in their own apartment. I was good at pretending.

I knew Domingo was a unique boy. He was barely sixteen and had taken on the responsibility of father and husband. He'd gotten real medical insurance so the baby and I would have good care and we wouldn't have to rely on the state's welfare system to pay for us. He worked harder than any grown man I knew—often eighty hours a week.

Because his father had not been in his life much, and he'd suffered as a child, I knew he would keep the promise he'd made the day I told him I was pregnant—that he would always care for our son. And he did. He loved his boy and was a good daddy—a proud and attentive daddy. We put Anthony between us in our bed, and Domingo would hold the baby's fingers and feet and say, "Look how perfect he is, Irene." Those times when it was the three of us together made me happy and gave me hope—hope that didn't last longer than the brief tender moments.

Prior to getting married, Domingo had promised my dad that I could go to cosmetology school and get my license. So when Anthony was nearly two years old, Domingo took me to sign up for school. I know he really didn't want me to go, but he had given his word to my dad, and Domingo always honored his word.

At the same time I started school, we rented a larger apartment. I was excited to have shag rugs and beautiful hardwood floors—ones

I scrubbed to a brilliant shine. I took a lot of pride in keeping my home shiny and neat.

Within a month of starting school, I discovered I was pregnant again. As crazy as it sounds, I was excited to have another child. It seemed like Domingo was meant to be a dad. And I thought maybe another child would change Domingo and he would stop drinking.

I put all my effort into school and began making big tips that helped with the greater expense of the larger apartment and gave us extra money as well. I enjoyed learning and treasured my growing independence. Mom watched Anthony while I worked. She was the perfect grandmother and loved her boy deeply.

Domingo's shop worked on catering trucks. Since the catering trucks had to be available during the day, the only time to do maintenance and repairs was at night. Domingo came home later and later. Soon he was also working on high-performance racing engines for cars. Being part of the racing circuit meant traveling on weekends. And it meant drinking, because drinking was an expected part of life in that world.

Our second son arrived a few days after I finished cosmetology school. I was glad Domingo was allowed to be in the delivery room with me this time. The excitement and joy when they laid Vincent next to me in that warm blanket were no less than I had felt with our first boy. I looked into this little boy's face and felt complete. I loved being a mom. And even with all the garbage between us, I knew Domingo's best role was as a dad.

In the course of three weeks I finished cosmetology school, had a baby, took my test, got my license, and landed a job at a decent salon. Then, when we were barely nineteen, we bought our first house—which surprised many family and friends. They couldn't believe we were able to do something so important when we were still so young.

Staying home and working on our house gave us both a powerful sense of pleasure. Domingo wasn't going out as much. We now had two beautiful boys who ran around and rode their bikes while Domingo mowed the lawn. Vincent adored being with his dad and seemed to be attached to his hip. In his little admiring eyes, his daddy could do no wrong. There was nothing more heartwarming than watching Domingo interact and play with his boys. When things got rough between us, I reminded myself what an excellent dad he was. I don't know why this soothed my heart and gave me hope, but it did.

As for me, these two little guys owned my heart. Every day with them was an adventure I looked forward to. They were so well behaved in public, such little gentlemen. But once they were home, their curiosity got them into much mischief. They especially liked to take things apart but weren't quite as adept at putting them back together.

Life at home could be really good at times. We'd visit family or go to the park. We went to the drive-in movies so the boys could be with us as much as possible. On the outside we looked like a normal, happy family, and there were moments I could almost feel like we were. But I had an odd split inside me. I resented my husband. I really did. And yet my heart melted when we went to the park and

I watched him play with our sons. For those brief moments I could believe that we were a good family and Domingo was a good man. During those special times I didn't want to admit to myself that I was getting really good at pretending. But my little fantasies didn't last. It wasn't more than a few days before the results of Domingo's alcoholism shattered them. No one knew the truth about the violence, but as often as he came after me, he never, ever, laid a hand on his sons. But Domingo's drinking had become obvious to my family, and our friends saw enough that they wondered how we stayed married.

Eventually Domingo got involved in building engines for the boat-racing circuit and started drinking more heavily. He was gone frequently, including most weekends, usually leaving the boys and me behind. I certainly didn't mind. I preferred it. It gave me a chance to breathe and have a break from the results of his drinking.

Our fights reminded me of birth pangs—they were getting stronger and closer together and were almost always physical. A rage built inside me, and at times I couldn't contain it. I was making good money at the salon, which gave me a sense of independence. I started thinking I could make it on my own. As far as I was concerned, it was only a matter of time before I would be out from under him and his controlling ways.

chapter 4

the struggle

When I first started working as a hairstylist, a shampoo and set cost three dollars and fifty cents. Within two years, I moved to a large corporate salon and quickly achieved my goal of becoming a master stylist. At the same time, our country was going through some big changes. The feminist movement began. I learned about women's rights—that life could be much different from what I had thought. I had choices! Imagine! A woman could do what she wanted without asking her husband! When *Roe v. Wade* was decided, the women in the salon cheered.

I felt as though my vision had cleared. I was no longer a naive sixteen-year-old girl; I was in my twenties, changing, a grown woman. I now knew my marriage was not something to be proud of. I admitted to myself that I was unhappy. I wanted to live a normal, happy life. I didn't need Domingo anymore. I felt stronger making my own money and receiving constant affirmation in my work. Doing very well in my own world gave me confidence in other areas of my life. I decided to get more education to better serve my clientele—traveling to workshops to learn different techniques—which meant my client list expanded and my books were full. By the time I was twenty-four I was making twenty-five dollars for a simple haircut and doing hair for movie and television stars as well as studio work.

I was on top of the world. But my deepest heart was empty and my soul lacking. And I was searching. For what, I didn't know. But I was looking to the world in hopes of finding it. My home life was a wreck and getting worse. At times I didn't care. I knew I was going to get a divorce anyway; I just needed to make more money. My life was going to change; it was just a matter of time.

One morning I didn't feel well. At the breakfast table, nausea swept through me. I knew I had to be pregnant. I didn't want another child. I loved my boys, but our life was a mess. All Domingo and I did was fight. So I considered getting an abortion. A week later, I was in the hospital having emergency surgery for a ruptured tubular pregnancy. God not only took my child, but the damage was so great, the resulting surgery guaranteed I would never be able to have another baby. I wish I could say that my heart was broken at the loss. It wasn't. Inside I was quietly rejoicing.

Domingo continued to drink, and the physical altercations got worse. I was so afraid of him when he got drunk. I did whatever he told me, hoping he wouldn't get mad and hit me.

I wondered, where was God? Why wasn't he helping us? I tried to be a good Catholic girl, faithfully attending church and taking

Communion. I prayed a lot. In the resulting silence I wondered if my parents had deceived me. Maybe there wasn't really a God.

I felt stuck in my marriage. My family loved Domingo, and many people admired him. In my pride, I wanted out but didn't want anyone to know about my imperfect wreck of a life. I felt there was no hope. All the while, the bitterness inside me grew like a cancer, taking over any good thought I might have had about Domingo.

I couldn't hide my seething hatred and anger from the boys. Besides, they heard us fighting—and I was not quiet about how I felt, so they heard all the ugly, horrible words I spewed at their father.

Domingo was always sorry when he sobered up. It was like living with Dr. Jekyll and Mr. Hyde. The funny thing was, I knew his apologies were sincere, so I forgave him and foolishly believed that this time things had changed. That it would never happen again. Many have asked me, "Why did you stay?" I can only say I really believed he would change. And I believed there was someone special deep down inside.

In that same deep place I felt Domingo loved me. And I didn't want to hurt him by leaving—he had been hurt so much in his life. What I really wanted was for us to stay married and be happy. In the back of my mind, I thought that if I could show him I could take care of me and the boys, then he would change.

When the boys were about five and seven, I gathered my tiny bit of courage, sucked up my pride, and moved out one weekend while

Domingo was away. I'd found a little apartment not too far from work that was perfect for the three of us.

After I'd put a deposit on the apartment, I told my parents, but very little, still feeling the need to protect Domingo. They loved him, but I think they knew what was going on.

When Domingo came home and found a partially empty house, he was outraged. He got my new number from my mom and called me right away, wanting to come over. I could tell he had been drinking, so I told him no. I felt a sense of freedom I'd never had. It felt good to be a working adult, on my own, in my own place. For the first time in years, I was not afraid. Every night I could go to bed without fearing I'd be awakened by an angry man. I didn't feel the ocean of anger pushing at me to say things I was ashamed of. As I drove to work, I knew for the first time that I was Irene Garcia and I was in charge of my life. I was capable of taking care of my boys.

Then one day Domingo came over and I let him in. He stomped in and demanded I come home. Instead of being afraid, I felt sorry for him. For once, I didn't say awful things back to him. His voice softened, and he told me he would no longer hurt me. I asked him to leave and told him that if he wanted to see us, he had to come sober.

Domingo honored my request. We had some really good times in my apartment. In fact, he went a long time without drinking. Yet I knew it was hard for him, especially when we went out on a date; he would have to drop me off and go home to a house without his family.

After six months of being separated, thinking that starting over might help, we decided to sell our house and buy another one. Domingo promised not to drink and hurt me anymore. We made money on the sale of our house, so we had extra funds to do fun things with the boys. Over the next two years we went to amusement parks, Hawaii, and Acapulco. I now looked forward to the weekends when Domingo was home rather than dreading them. I stopped working Saturdays so we could have concentrated family time. It finally seemed as though we were going to make it.

broken nose

One Sunday afternoon, when we were getting ready to go to a family barbecue, I noticed that Domingo had already started drinking. I wanted so badly not to say a word and keep quiet, but rage and anger took over and the fight began. In my stupid thinking, I felt it would be wrong to go down without a fight. Besides, I was determined to become stronger and not continue to be the weak person I hated.

"*I hate your guts!*" I screamed at him, then added a few cuss words. "I'm so embarrassed of you. I don't want you to go with us. I'm going with the boys without you."

The next moment I saw stars. Pain surged through my face, and blood was everywhere. As Domingo pressed towels against my face, the taste of blood went down my throat. When my vision cleared, I saw a look of panic on Domingo's face. When I looked in the mirror, I knew why. Panic filled me as well. All I could think was, *How am I going to explain this one?*

As we silently sat side by side in the emergency room, I ran ideas through my head. If I told the doctor what really happened, he would call the police to arrest Domingo. I looked over at Domingo and felt sorry for him as he sat there, slumped over, looking devastated, even though I was the one bleeding. Misery consumed him.

When they took me in and asked what happened, I told them I was playing softball and got hit in the nose. My nose had been broken in three places. It needed immediate attention, so they scheduled surgery for the next morning.

When I woke up from the anesthesia, the doctor told me that he had discovered I also had an old break that had left scar tissue and that he had tended to that as well. He didn't ask when the other break had happened, and I was glad. I had no idea since it could have been any number of times. And would he have believed the same story twice? I doubt it.

Domingo sat next to me, still looking miserable. I knew he was sorry. I could see it on his face and throughout his entire body. We never talked about some of those things, the times when he hurt me worse than others. When I screamed horrible things at him, I attacked his character and mocked him, but I never threw at him the things he had done to me—because I was fearful he would do them again.

I was so stupid. As scared as I was of him hurting me, you'd think I would have kept my mouth shut. Somehow, I guess I thought yelling at him would put up a protective wall between us—that I could hurt him with my words as much as he hurt me with his fists.

And I did hurt him. Deeply. And sometimes my words were what triggered his fists and his rage. My words sometimes simmered inside him when he was sober. Adding alcohol to the thoughts brought out his physical attacks. We had a vicious cycle neither of us was willing to break. One would hurt the other, and the other would lash back. Today, neither of us excuses our behavior back then. There was no excuse for what we did to each other.

a mystery

One night, after I'd covered Domingo's untouched dinner and put it in the refrigerator, I went to bed, knowing it was shaping up to be a bad night. He usually called me before he left the shop so I could either prepare his dinner or get it reheated. When he didn't call or didn't show up when he said he'd be home, I'd either put his dinner in a warm oven or in the refrigerator, knowing he was most likely drinking and wouldn't be home until the middle of the night. I dreaded those nights. And the later it got, the worse I knew it would be.

On nights like those, I knew his rage would be at the surface, so I tried not to speak a word when he got home. I usually ignored him, pretending to sleep. If I did speak, I'd pay for it.

Things had gotten much worse in our marriage. Domingo had moved from beer to hard liquor. This seemed to bring a deeper, meaner drunk out in him. When he came home like that, his face, especially his eyes, making him look like a man possessed by some sort of pure evil. It didn't take much to throw him into a rage. A shoe left out. A boy's bike outside the garage. His dinner not prepared.

I can almost taste and feel that day. I'd been thinking about our marriage, wondering why he was mad at me all the time. I was dumbfounded. It seemed as though nothing I ever did made him happy. There were so many times when it didn't make sense for him to be angry with me. Why was he mad when we went somewhere for a fun gathering with family? Or at the park with the boys? What about when we went on trips? I could pretend to be happy, so why couldn't he? I fed him, washed his clothes, took care of our boys, worked hard at an outside job.

I really loved my role as wife and mother. I didn't love *him*, but I loved my role. Cooking and caring for my family brought me great pleasure.

There was an overwhelming tension growing between us that I knew was a sign of bad things to come. This night Domingo had promised to come home early enough to spend time with us. But he never showed. He'd called and told me he'd be home at seven for dinner. By eight, we knew he wasn't coming. And by nine, I knew the night wasn't going to end well. Unless I could pretend I was asleep.

I tucked the boys in and then went to bed, partly because I had to work the next day.

The moment he walked through the door at 2:30 a.m., I prayed, *Lord, let him just go to bed. Please.*

He marched into the bedroom, furious. My head pounded and my heart thumped. This was going to be a bad one. I pretended to be asleep, but he didn't buy it. "So, Irene," he yelled, "what were you doing tonight? Who were you with?" Accusations poured out of his mouth. It seemed as though every other word was a profanity. Often an ugly, degrading term for me and what he thought of me.

Fear began to swell within, taking over my entire body.

"What did you do today?" he demanded again. "Who were you with?"

You would think after all I'd been through that I'd be quiet. But *no*. I sat up in my bed and spewed out the most vile and wicked words back. "I was at work the whole day, Domingo. I'm with my kids. I'm where *I'm* supposed to be, but you weren't where *you* were supposed to be, and you're calling *me* vile things? Who do you think you are? You *know* I'm faithful."

He turned on the light in the bathroom, and the glow lit his face. I saw a storm brewing inside him like I'd never seen before. His eyes didn't look like his eyes. Fear poured through me. I feared for my life. I knew it was over. This was the last time he'd hurt me—because I was going to die.

"I'm going to teach you, Irene," he said, seething. "I'm going to give you what you deserve. *I'll* show you who I am."

Silently I prayed, *Dear God, help me. Please protect me.* Just as I finished praying, Domingo turned slightly to come at me, and I heard a loud crack.

What was that?

He collapsed to the ground. My first thought was that it sounded like his leg had broken, but my second thought was that there was no way that could have happened.

I could tell he'd passed out, so I left him there on the floor, thankful he had been kept from hurting me. I knew I was safe for the rest of the night, so I fell asleep. How I was able to fall asleep so quickly, I don't know. Was I exhausted after the surge of fear? Was God giving me grace?

When I woke early the next morning, he was still in the same place. As I stepped around him to get ready to go to work, he looked up and said, "I can't walk, Irene. I'm in a lot of pain."

My kind, compassionate self responded with "That's what you get." I was no longer afraid. Now I was just mad. I had no sympathy. All I could think about was getting to work on time, so I slipped around the wall that hid our bathroom from the main part of the bedroom to get ready.

"Irene," his pathetic voice called. "Will you get the boys?"

"In a minute."

I wrapped the cord around the blow-dryer and tucked it into the drawer of the cabinet. I took one last look in the mirror and stepped into the hallway, calling the boys, who came right away. I wasn't the least bit concerned about the pain Domingo was in. I reveled in the fact he was hurting, so I took my time.

"What's wrong, Dad?" the boys both asked.

"Mingo," I said, not answering them, "your truck is blocking my car."

He fished inside his pocket and handed over the keys.

Just to be mean and vindictive, I drove the truck down the street and left it there. I walked back to the house, dropped off his keys, got my purse and keys, and quickly left.

All the way to work a voice in the back of my mind kept saying, *His leg is broken, his leg is broken*. And another voice chanted back, *No, it's not, no, it's not*. How could it possibly be broken? He hadn't *done* anything. He hadn't even made an eighth of a turn. He hadn't wheeled around. He'd barely turned to take a step toward me. There was no way it was broken.

But he was in so much pain. Why?

Nothing made sense, so I pushed it all out of my mind.

Later I learned he was in so much pain that the boys had to help him up. Because he couldn't walk, he used each boy as a crutch to hobble all the way down the street to get his truck, his leg wobbling worthlessly. Domingo pulled himself up into the truck, put his leg on the seat next to him, and drove himself and the boys to the hospital with his left foot.

Sometime around noon, I got a call at work. "Irene," Domingo said, "I'm at the hospital. My leg is broken in three places. There are two breaks in the tibia and one in the fibula."

"Are you sure? You sure the doctors didn't make a mistake?"

"No, Irene. There's no mistake. I saw the X-rays. They're clearly broken."

Fear grabbed me, and I wondered if he'd be able to go to work. I'd become so distant from my husband that all I cared about was whether he could continue to support us.

When I got home, Domingo was lying on the couch, his leg in a full cast up to his thigh. He told me the doctors were running tests because they said it was impossible for his leg to break from such a slight turn. Later, when we told people what happened, no one really believed us. I think everyone thought I hit him with a baseball bat. Believe me, if I'd had a bat that night, I would have used it. But I never touched him, and he never touched me.

After he apologized for what he'd said to me, we never talked about the incident again.

Because he was laid up and couldn't move around much, I had to wait on him. On the one hand, I was miserable every minute of it. I didn't want to be kind. On the other hand, I enjoyed it, because it was hard on him to sit back and have a woman do what he should have been able to do for himself. I liked my new position and used every bit of it to my advantage.

After the long weekend, my uncomplaining husband was up and moving about. And he never missed a day of work. The cast slowed him down physically, but his drinking didn't slow a bit.

This event sealed it for me. I was going to work harder at the salon so I could leave my husband for good. I could feel a big change rumbling in the distance. I could almost see it on the horizon. I knew what it would look like, and that knowledge gave me a quiet satisfaction. We would be divorced. And I would be done with him forever.

chapter 5

when God steps in

A beautiful woman of about forty years sat in my salon chair. She was extremely feminine—attractive but dressed modestly. She asked for a simple style and haircut. She wanted to look nice for her husband and sons.

From that first day, I knew she was different from any other woman I had ever met, radiating something I had never seen before. She reminded me of Mrs. Cleaver from *Leave It to Beaver*— soft-spoken, with a positive outlook on everyone and everything. She was confident about life and had strong moral convictions. Being brought up in a traditional Mexican Catholic home, I, too, had moral convictions. What I didn't have—but wanted—was her joy and peace, the inner beauty that made her shine.

Her name was Mary Barshaw, and before long I was telling her things I had told no one else. I trusted her completely. She never judged me; she just kept on loving me, no matter what ugliness I revealed to her about myself. "It's okay, honey," she'd say in her sweet voice, patting my arm. "Jesus forgives you." Usually clients confide in their hairdressers, but this time the hairdresser was confiding in her client. We talked about my marriage, or my children, and she helped me with parenting ideas. Or she shared wisdom about life. I looked forward to her weekly visits.

One day Mary invited me to her home for lunch. She had already invited me several times, and each time, at the last minute, I had canceled. This time I decided it would be rude not to show up and forced myself to go ahead with it.

When I got there, I found it odd that her husband, Fred, was there in the middle of the day. Mary explained, "I asked Fred if he could be here because you have so many questions about God."

I smiled and shook his hand but felt uncomfortable with him there. I had hoped to be alone with Mary.

It didn't take long to see how much they loved each other. Their interaction was genuine and loving. And I was also taken aback to hear the way they spoke so freely about God and his Son, Jesus. But as we sat at the table, eating the wonderful lunch she had lovingly prepared, I relaxed. They were kind and gentle with me, and I felt safe. And seemed like they could answer every question I could think to ask about God and the Bible. I was very impressed and became comfortable, and our conversation lasted for at least an hour.

Then Mary stood to clear the table, leaving me alone with Fred, who started asking me strange questions. By then I was okay being alone with him. Besides, I presumed Mary would return at any moment to sit with us.

"Do you believe in God?" he asked.

That question bewildered me. "Of course I do. I told you I'm Catholic."

"Do you have a personal relationship with Christ?"

I had no idea what he meant. His words went right over my head. Probably noticing that I didn't have a clue what he was talking about, he asked me another question. "Do you want to be a follower of Christ?"

That's what Mary had been talking to me about at the salon. But I was still confused. How was any of this different from everything I'd believed and done as a Catholic?

"Jesus died on the cross for every person," Fred explained, "because we're all sinners. God hates sin, and there must be a sacrifice for it."

I got that. I went to confession all the time. I knew a lot about sin. I committed a lot of sins too. Especially with my mouth.

"Because Jesus was crucified on the cross, his blood can be the sacrifice so your sins can be cleansed and erased and you can receive eternal life."

I nodded, not because I understood, because I didn't—it was still over my head—but because that's what you do when you're listening to someone, even if you don't get it.

"All you need to do, Irene, is to acknowledge that you're a sinner, ask God for forgiveness, and confess with your mouth that Jesus is Lord of your life. This means you will obey and follow Jesus."

I've never claimed to be an intellect. I'm a simple woman. So it was hard for me to understand what all his words meant. But I knew I wanted what the two of them had—that whatever it was was really good. Then Fred asked if he could pray.

I bowed my head, and as he prayed, I silently repeated the words he said in his prayer. When he said, "Amen," I wasn't sure what was supposed to have happened. I didn't understand that he had presented the gospel. I didn't understand that I had done, in my heart, the thing that would now make me a Christian—I made Jesus Lord of my life. I don't think it was important that I clearly understood. What I *did* know was that I wanted, with all my heart, to have peace with God. To have a connection with God through Jesus. So if that's what Fred was saying with all those words and concepts I couldn't understand, then that's truly what I wanted.

When we opened our eyes, I realized I had gotten so caught up with what Fred was telling me that I didn't notice Mary had not come back. I never did ask her where she had been, but I can bet she was in the next room praying for my salvation.

I thanked them both for lunch and said I needed to leave. I didn't even think to tell either of them that I'd repeated Fred's prayer—and meant it.

Not long after that, I changed salons, and Mary could no longer afford to come to me to get her hair done. So she didn't know I had become a Christian that day.

No one knew I was now a believer. I was trying to grow the best I could, but I was discouraged with all my fumbling. So I called Mary and told her that if she would come in every week to talk with me, I would do her hair for free. I didn't know then about older women teaching younger women as the Bible talks about in the book of Titus; I just knew I needed help, and I knew she could give it. She agreed and discipled me for over thirty years.

hungry

I was eager to learn all I could about God, but it seemed that the more I tried to get close to God, the more Domingo drank. But he was traveling a lot on the racing circuit—one year he was gone forty-six weekends—so things got a little easier at home. This meant the boys and I were alone and did everything together. On Sundays we started going to church where the Barshaws went—Grace Community Church, where the pastor-teacher, John MacArthur, was teaching verse by verse through the New Testament book of Matthew. I was in awe that anyone could teach so much out of one verse. It was a great book for a beginner like me to study because it was filled with Jesus's teachings and had great applications for my life.

Little by little, God also revealed his truths to me through Mary. She faithfully met with me week after week, gently showing me my faults. She taught me that as long as I focused on Domingo's sin, I looked pretty good. It was not until I compared myself to Christ that I could see how filthy I really was.

As a Catholic, I hadn't really opened my Bible much. But John MacArthur's teaching inspired me to get mine out and look into it more deeply. As I did, it was clear that God wanted Christians to be married to Christians. And since I was now a Christian, I believed God wanted me to be with a Christian husband. So, in my naive thinking, I believed God was going to give me a new husband. I just had to keep praying for him—whoever he might be. I dreamed of having a family who went to church together like the families I saw sitting together in the Catholic church when I was a child.

By this time it was no secret how I felt about my husband. I knew he wasn't faithful. My heart ached with this knowledge every time he was away. In my stupidity and ignorance, I prayed continually, "God, take this man. Let him drive over the cliff and die on the way home. And give me a Christian husband." My foolish prayers are very hard for me to admit. How dare I pray God would take my husband's life!

Boy, do I thank God for the Holy Spirit, who is the mediator of our prayers, perfecting them. Romans 8:26–27 says, "And the Holy Spirit helps us in our weakness. For example, we don't know what God wants us to pray for. But the Holy Spirit prays for us with groanings that cannot be expressed in words. And the Father who knows all hearts knows what the Spirit is saying, for the Spirit pleads for us believers in harmony with God's own will."

These verses tell me that there are times we might not know how to pray, but the Spirit perfects our prayers and aligns them with God's will. So while I prayed fervently for my unbelieving husband's death, I believe the Holy Spirit changed my words so God heard, "Please, Lord, save my husband and make him a new man in Christ."

One day Domingo didn't come home. No one knew where he was. I knew one of three things had happened: he was with another woman, he'd gone off a canyon cliff because he had been drinking, or he'd gotten a DUI. He'd already had one DUI, and I told him if he ever got a second, our marriage was over.

When Domingo called to tell me he'd been picked up on a DUI on the freeway off-ramp close to our house, I was so humiliated and so done. All I could think was, *Why is he still alive?* Then he told me he was going to be in jail for a few days.

I didn't care. I was filing for divorce. I thought God wanted me to be free of this awful man who was drunk and angry much of the time. While he went to jail, I went on with my life and my plans for divorce, never visiting him in jail or even caring that he was there.

Domingo's story in his own words

I could see our house from where the cops pulled me over—only one block away. After failing the sobriety test, I appealed to the police to let me leave the truck there and walk home. After all, I was so close. "Does it really matter?" I asked. "Look, see that house? I live there. You can impound my car, whatever you want, but please just let me walk home."

"No, Mr. Garcia," the cop said. "This isn't your first DUI. We're taking you in."

I can't believe it. It's just my rotten luck that I get pulled over a block from my house, I thought as they handcuffed me, adding to my humiliation, then put me in the backseat of the police car.

I didn't want to call Irene.

We had battled so long over my drinking, and as a result, our marriage had turned volatile. I knew Irene no longer wanted to live this way. I didn't want to tell her about the DUI—I knew it would be the last straw and calling her would mean the end of our relationship. She had already been thinking about a divorce. But I had to call. And when I did, I could hear the disgust in her voice.

Wait until she hears I have to spend a week in jail.

When it was time to go to jail, I drove myself because I didn't want to bother anyone or answer a bunch of questions. I parked across the street, hoping my truck would be okay since the jail wasn't in a great neighborhood.

I hated jail. I hated being in a big room with my back against a wall. Then to be stuck with all those bums—losers who couldn't even hold down a job. The first day I looked around and thought, I don't belong here. There's just a bunch of scum here. I'm a corporate vice president, while these guys are just a bunch of losers. I bet they don't even work. I own my own home. A boat. Two new cars. What can they say about what they have achieved in life? Nothing. Plain old nothing.

About halfway through the second day I thought, Well, some of these guys are okay. But I still don't belong here. These guys live in and out of this place. I just had a little bad luck. I'm only here because of the dirty cops who had it out for me.

I spent the next few hours thinking about that. I'd been raised in a culture where the cops were the bad guys, the enemy, the people who made our lives miserable and interrupted our fun with all their stupid rules. I had no respect for any cops—especially the cops who had arrested me.

There wasn't anything to do in jail except sit and think, and I wasn't used to that. Outside of jail I felt like I had to keep moving, always going a hundred miles an hour, busy accomplishing important things, while these guys were used to sitting around doing nothing. I had never stopped to think about what I was doing, or more importantly why. I probably hadn't sat still like that since I was a kid sitting on the curb, watching the other kids play ball and deciding that God, like the cops, was unfair.

By the third day, I realized the cops had only been doing their job. They were only trying to keep the streets safe. Since I don't even remember driving that night before being pulled over, I must have been pretty bad off. But I still don't deserve this.

Then God humbled me to where I admitted to myself that it wasn't really their fault—it was mine because I drink.

Why do I drink?

Well, that was obviously my brother's and cousin's fault. They got me started when I was eleven, putting a beer in my hand every opportunity they could. All the guys who came to the shop brought me beer too. Everyone I knew and worked with drank. It was just what we did.

On the fourth day, I thought about how it really wasn't my brother's or brother-in-law's or cousin's fault. I chose to drink.

Why?

The only time I really felt happy was when I drank. It was the only time I felt okay. I was free and at ease when I was drunk.

By the fifth day, I knew the real reason I drank was to try to forget my childhood. It was my only escape from those horrible memories. They haunted and tormented me. I could understand why my sister drank. There were memories she would never talk about. And my brother had been injured in a horrifying accident as a child. Because my father would not take him to the doctor, this young, energetic boy became paralyzed on the right side of his body for the rest of his life. He, too, drank excessively.

As I faced my childhood memories, I realized one of the things that hurt me so much was that my dad wasn't there for me as a child—wasn't there for any of us children. And there were so many things my family suffered.

Then it hit me like a ton of bricks. I was doing the same thing to my boys that my dad had done to me. I was never there for them. I was always working, traveling, and drinking. They were watching me treat Irene the way I had watched my dad treat my mom, which I hated to see as a child. I was doing the same things my dad did and, to my best memory, his dad had done as well.

Funny thing was, sitting there stuck in that jail, I finally got that I was running and hiding from myself. Sitting still forced me to think about my sins. The pain and damage I had caused to those I loved. I was miserable. I hated what I had become.

As I think back on those days, I hear the apostle Paul: "I want to do what is right, but I don't do it. Instead, I do what I hate" (Rom. 7:15). I hated what I did and who I became when I drank. And that really wasn't who I was deep inside. I believe Irene knew that too, and that's why she stayed for so long.

I felt sorry for Irene and what I had done to her, but I was caught in this endless downward spiral, generation after generation, headed straight to hell. I didn't want my kids and my grandkids to live out that same hurt. I wanted to stop it. I wanted to change. I wanted a new start at life, a do-over. I'd made a mess of my life, and I was going to live out the rest for God.

I had tried to stop drinking in the past, and it hadn't worked—at least not for long. I knew I couldn't do it on my own. I needed God's help, the same God I had said was unfair and I didn't want to have anything to do with. But I had nowhere else to go for the kind of help I needed. So I prayed—or should I say bargained with God: "Okay, I surrender. If you take away my desire to drink, restore my family, I will follow you. Wherever it takes me. Whatever that means, I will do it."

I knew I really didn't know what that meant, but whatever it was, I was going to do it.

When I finished my prayer, I instantly knew something was different. I wasn't sure what it was, or if it was for real. It was like a huge weight had been taken off my shoulders. I felt free!

At that moment, my name came over the loudspeaker. I was getting out. When I went outside, I found that my truck had been stripped. Normally I would have been furious about someone tampering with my Black Beauty. Now I was just glad it still ran.

I drove down the steep hill from the old Ventura County Jail to Highway 101 to go home. I could see the ocean—it was huge and open. I wasn't meant to be boxed in.

And then it came to me. Today is the first day of the rest of my life. I'd heard the phrase before, but it had no meaning to me then. It was stupid and cliché and sounded good to the people who were saying it. But now, for me, it was a powerful, freeing truth.

I went home to be with those who loved me and prayed they would forgive me for the pain I had caused them.

forgiveness? are you crazy?

"Just a minute, Mary," I said, putting my comb and scissors down to answer the phone.

"Irene."

It was Domingo. He sounded broken, ashamed. But I had made up my mind. Our marriage was done. I was done. I wanted a new beginning. I was beaten down, exhausted, and tired of fighting. I didn't want to say terrible things anymore. I wanted to change and make God proud of me. I wanted to be restored.

But, even though I didn't want to admit it, I was going to miss Domingo. After all, we'd been together ten years. I would miss the Domingo who was soft and caring. The father of my boys.

I wanted to slam the phone down, not because I was angry, but because I was heartbroken.

"Irene," he said, his voice soft yet full of conviction, "I know you're leaving me. I know you want a divorce. But you just gotta hear me out." He spoke slowly and methodically. "We've been married for ten years. In those ten years I've given you the worst years of my life, and it's probably the worst my life will ever be.

"I'm a new man now. I will never drink again. I'm going to be somebody different. Do you want the new me? Or do you want someone else to have me? I feel you deserve the best years of my life. If you leave now, you'll have only had my worst years, and someone else is going to get the best of me. But I believe it should be you. Do you want me to be someone different to someone else? Or will you forgive me?"

My emotions flipped to anger. I wanted to scream, "How dare you say you're going to go with someone else and you're going to give her those good years I deserved!" Instead, I quietly hung up and grabbed the comb and scissors so I could finish Mary's haircut.

"You're not going to believe this, Mary," I said. "That was Domingo." I proceeded to share with her what he'd said.

"Honey," Mary said in her soft, sweet voice, "he's asking you to forgive him. You have to forgive him."

"Mary, I can't forgive my husband. Come on!"

She gently grabbed my hand, stopping me from working on her hair. "Honey," she said again, "God hates divorce. You must forgive your husband because he is asking for you to forgive him."

Angry words flooded my brain. I wanted to snap at her, "Lady, you come from your little kumbaya world with your little Christian friends, and you don't really know what my life is about. So don't you sit there and tell me I have to forgive him. I don't have to forgive him." But I clamped my mouth shut and didn't say a word.

On my drive home, I was still upset. "Why, Lord?" I asked. "Why do I have to forgive him? It's not right."

I wrestled with God the entire way home. I wanted a different life. I didn't deserve all of this. "Please, God," I pleaded as I maneuvered through rush-hour traffic. "Don't make me forgive my husband."

Then God spoke to me. "Irene, I stretched my arms out like this—not only for you, but for Domingo, too."

I could instantly see the arms of Jesus stretched out on the cross. I felt so ashamed. I wasn't any better than Domingo. I was as much of a sinner as he was—just in different ways. Jesus died for me, and I gladly accepted his forgiveness. How could I not forgive my husband when Jesus already had? God forgave me, so I had to forgive my husband.

I knew the right thing to do, but it was so hard. I needed to trust God. I had to obey him. For me there was no other choice.

a new start

You'd think I'd have been excited about a new start for us, but the truth was, I still didn't love Domingo. Nor did I fully trust him. I couldn't erase ten years of ugliness overnight and still resented that God had not brought me a new husband. It didn't take long to see that God was already working in my husband's heart, truly making him a new creature. But my heart remained stone-cold. In the beginning, I forced myself to pray that God would heal my heart and teach me to love my husband. In time, it became easier. Eventually the prayers became the honest plea of my heart.

While he was sitting in jail, Domingo had asked God to help him be a good husband and father. And he knew that in order to get his family back, he would have to mend a lot of relationships—especially the one with our elder son. Anthony and I were very close, and he wanted to protect me, so he, too, struggled with hatred for his dad. We found out later that he was outside our bedroom door, bargaining with God, the night Domingo's leg broke. He told God he would commit his life to him if God would protect me. When I think of the pain and anguish we caused our boys, I shudder.

Domingo made some immediate changes in his life. First he quit racing, and then he told his brother-in-law he would work only forty hours a week. If his brother-in-law wasn't okay with those hours, then Domingo would find another job. His brother-in-law agreed to accept Domingo's new hours.

True to his word, when five o'clock came around and the racers rolled in with cases of beer, Domingo rolled out. No one understood his new behavior. What was wrong with hanging out and drinking a few beers? Domingo knew that in order to completely change, he had to change his friends and habits completely.

Domingo also started listening to the tapes I brought home from church. He was still not a Christian and was reluctant to go to church. His memories of all the phonies he'd seen in church were too persistent for him to ignore. But he listened to those tapes as he drove. A year or so later, he promised he'd start going to church with me. And he did.

The Sunday he came for the first time, I was so excited. I kept looking at Domingo and smiling. We were going to church as a *family*. My long-ago dream was becoming a reality. I warmed and rejoiced inside because God had answered my many prayers.

Sometime after that, he gave his life to Christ and completely surrendered. And then Domingo's faith took off. That day was the beginning of a new life for the Garcias.

I must admit it has been difficult to write these things about Domingo, because he is no longer the man he was before he quit drinking. But I write them so people can see how God can take two wicked hearts and turn them his way.

I had been so busy looking at Domingo's behavior that I took my eyes off the cross. When I understood that it's God's business to change hearts, not mine, and that I had to work on me and not Domingo, I stood back and let God do the changing. I finally understood that my job was to pray for my husband, encourage him, and not Bible beat him. That was when the change in him really began to show.

Years later, when my husband shared his testimony about this time in our lives, he said, "I knew there had to be a God when my wife kept her mouth shut." He was right. It was God's doing. I was learning many things about the power of God and realized I had the power in Christ to overcome the obstacles I faced in every area of my life.

The beautiful thing was, God answered a prayer I had been praying for years. He gave me the new husband I wanted—only it was Domingo. I shudder when I think of my plan to leave my husband and that I prayed for God to take Domingo's life. I'm extremely thankful that God worked a miracle and that I am still married to the same boy I fell in love with at the drinking fountain so long ago.

honeymoon years

All of a sudden I felt as though I was the most important person in the world to Domingo. The dark veil seemed to have been torn away from his eyes, and I felt beautiful for the first time in my life. There were times when I walked into Domingo's work unexpectedly, our eyes would meet, and he would glow.

We started to date and spend a lot of time together. We went out to dinner. We bought a new family boat and went waterskiing a lot, and I learned how to ride dirt and street motorcycles so I could keep up with all three of my boys. We went on vacations, played, and got to know each other. Even staying home was wonderful.

My boys began to build a relationship with their dad. When they worked together in the garage, I could hear them laughing and joking around. He taught them how to build and repair things. One time they built a dune buggy, then went exploring our hills. We spent hours at the dinner table, laughing and enjoying each other. While I cleaned up, these three boys planned Garcia adventures.

Best of all, there was no longer a dark cloud over our family. I was married to a man who loved me. My boys were thriving. I didn't feel I deserved their love after I'd put them through so much hell. Yet miraculously they forgave me. And their dad.

Then the unthinkable happened. I fell in love with my husband. He had become the most important person in my life—my best friend. I was content and felt so safe. Safe! With *my* husband! I looked forward to spending time with him. His body language spoke loudly—I was the one he wanted to be with, and most of all, I was the one he loved. I know there was a newlywed glow inside me. To love and be loved is an incredible gift from God.

We were all blown away by the changes occurring in Domingo. I was so proud of him. And I sensed his pride in me. I will always count those years as the best in my life. I love my life now, but that was a very special time. We went from the deepest darkness of hatred and meanness to the bright light of love, excitement, and joy. It's sad to think we were married for over ten years and were only then getting to know each other. Still, I thank God for our belated honeymoon. It was then my broken heart was healed.

The word *perseverance* came to me often during those honeymoon years, and still does. God taught me what it means to persevere through the darkness when all hope has been lost, when it seems as though there will never be a positive outcome. It took many years, it wasn't easy, it took trusting and obeying God even when it felt like the wrong thing to do, but joy and remarkable change did come. But I had to persevere to find that out.

And I would desperately need that lesson in the years to come.

PART 2

COMPASSIONATE

♡

chapter 6

Esther

1981

My life was filled to overflowing with love and happiness, and I was continually rejoicing in the many blessings God had given me. Yet, in another part of me, an emptiness began to grow. I believe it was the Spirit nudging me toward the next step in our lives.

I was beginning to get lonely with the boys constantly at their dad's side. I wanted so badly to have a baby girl. Someone I could pass down all the things my mom taught me and her mom taught her.

I talked with Mary Barshaw about my desire to adopt a girl and that I didn't think Domingo would ever consider it. She encouraged me to share my heart with Domingo, so I did. She also told me that if God had put the desire in my heart, it would happen. That thought excited me. Later I shared my desires with Domingo. He was not happy about my idea, but he listened.

"I don't want to be tied down with a baby, Irene. We're having so much fun with the boys. They're at a good age to get out and do so many things. Think of all the things we're doing. Do you really want to be tied down?"

"Okay, Mingo," I said, trying not to let on how disappointed I was. I knew he was right, but nothing could take away my deep desire for a little girl.

Then one morning, as I handed him his coffee, he said, "Go ahead and look into adopting a little girl."

"Are you kidding me, Mingo?" As someone who can't contain her emotions, I danced in circles. Then I hugged and kissed him. I was afraid he was going to change his mind, so I immediately started making calls.

About a month later we met our social worker, a kind woman who suffered from dwarfism. She shared the many struggles she encountered due to her disability. As she spoke, I could see she was making a connection with Domingo. I'm sure she saw his soft heart as he leaned forward, hanging on every word she said. He asked some questions, but mostly he listened. Then she moved on to tell us about our options. There was a big need for Mexican families to adopt, so we were put at the top of the adoption list. Within months we were qualified.

The agency brought us a questionnaire that asked what kind of child we wanted. We could check boxes next to what was important to us. The list was amazing. I felt like we were putting in an order to buy a child. It asked questions like: Would you take a child whose parents were drug addicts? Were illiterate? A child of mixed race? One who has siblings? Is hyperactive? Has tantrums? Is mentally disabled?

My only request was for a baby girl. I didn't care about anything else. Domingo, being more logical, thought it would be hard for us to take in certain children. We talked about it for a long time. We decided we could handle many disabilities in a child, but we couldn't sacrifice our new life to take in a mentally disabled child. So I agreed to request a healthy older girl as Domingo wanted—but the real truth was I wanted a baby, and I would take her regardless of her issues. We were told the waiting process for a child could take a few years, so we prepared to wait.

It didn't take nearly that long to receive the anticipated phone call. "I have a baby girl. She's six weeks old, is a failure-to-thrive baby, and there is a strong possibility she has brain damage."

I only heard *baby girl*, and Domingo only heard *brain damage*. When we got to the social worker's office, she told us that the baby's fourteen-year-old mother had been raped while in a foster home. The doctors thought the baby's issues were so severe that she wouldn't make it more than a year.

Then the social worker explained why she felt we should have this baby. She sounded like a salesman trying to talk Domingo into buying used goods. I sat there feeling nervous and sick, knowing how much Domingo did not want a mentally disabled child. I couldn't really hear their words. All I could hear was the thumping of my heart that also beat inside my head. I didn't want to say no to this baby. I thought this might be our only opportunity.

My natural bent would be to talk Domingo into my way of thinking. But this time I was smart enough to remain silent. I knew I couldn't make this decision for Domingo, nor pressure him into it. This was a decision that would impact the rest of our lives, and I didn't want either of us to have regrets. I had to honor Domingo, whatever the outcome. Still, I prayed he would change his mind.

"Before you decide," the social worker finally said, "I want you to meet her." (Smart woman!) She began to gather her things. "Why don't you two go get something to eat while I get the baby?"

At the restaurant, after our server put our plates of food in front of us, Domingo took my hand so he could pray and give thanks for our meal. He opened his mouth to speak—and then all of a sudden he stopped. He had a strange expression on his face. My heart dropped.

Oh no, here it comes, I thought. *He's going to tell me this isn't going to work. It's not the beginning like I'd hoped—it's the end.*

A rush of words came out of Domingo. "Oh, Irene. I see it now. Here I am professing to love God, but I'm saying no to him. That I don't want to take this innocent child. It's like God just hit me with a bat. I get it. She didn't ask to be born. She's an innocent victim. And I'm so selfish that I don't want to take her because it's inconvenient for me and my family. God is giving me a child. A beautiful gift. Who am I to say no?" He put his head down and took another deep breath before he looked at me and spoke again. "I have been so selfish with my family. I'm so ashamed."

Then he confessed that from the beginning he thought no one would give us a child because of our history. He figured that if he went along with the adoption, the agency would deny us and he wouldn't have to be the bad guy for saying no.

He continued. "While we were in the office, all my thoughts were about how I was going to graciously talk you out of taking this baby." Domingo grabbed my other hand. "Lord, forgive me for my selfish ways. Your Son died for me, and I was not willing to take this child. I promise you, Lord, from this day forward I will take care of this baby. If I have to push her in a wheelchair, walk for her, talk for her for the rest of her life, I will. I commit to provide, care, protect, and love her my whole life. Amen."

It took me a moment to get over the shock. Then excitement shot through me. Neither of us could eat now. We wanted to get back and meet our baby girl.

I couldn't believe how tiny this six-week-old baby was. She was this itty-bitty thing who weighed less than six pounds and was losing weight. She could have fit into a shoe box. She was precious and delicate. And so lethargic. A six-week-old baby should have had some sort of response to being held, and yet she had none. Tears rolled down our cheeks as we held her. My heart ached for this little baby. And yet I thanked God that her mother didn't get an abortion.

The social worker told us that most babies are easy to place, but this one couldn't be placed at all.

I didn't care what list she was on or what the world thought of her. This was my daughter, and she was perfect. To this day I tell Esther that she is more than I could have asked for—beautiful, truly a gift from God.

That didn't mean life with her was easy. Esther was very sick, but her dad kept his word. He held her and loved her continually. I used to get jealous because she wanted to be with him more than me.

We all loved her so much. The boys took her everywhere with them. I wanted to be with her all the time. This little thing was the center of the Garcia family.

One day when she was eighteen months old, she cried so hard she stopped breathing and lost consciousness. The boys called 911, and I panicked. I started mouth-to-mouth resuscitation. As I blew air into her tiny mouth, I was thinking, *Small, soft breaths, small, soft breaths,* but I was blowing as hard as I could. Nothing happened. She wasn't responding. In my panic, I picked her up and ran out of the house with no plan of what I was going to do. I guess I thought running was going to help. I ran to my neighbor's house and pounded on the door. The man opened the door, liquor on his breath. "My baby's not breathing," I said, then shoved her into his arms and ran in another direction.

I know it's crazy and doesn't make sense, but all I can say is that when your child isn't breathing, your brain cells leave your brain.

My neighbor put her on the floor, bent down, and gave her mouth-to-mouth. As I watched from a distance, panic still streaming through me, all I could think about was the liquor on his breath being pushed into my baby's lungs.

Finally the paramedics showed up.

I rode to the hospital in the back of the ambulance, wondering if she was going to die. "Domingo," I said, "why would God take our precious baby?"

"Irene," he said in his soft, controlled voice, "we need to be thankful we had her for over a year. She knew she was loved. She is God's child, and he can do whatever he wants with her."

I was astounded that this was *my* husband talking—the one who had been a Christian for only a little less than two years.

At the hospital, the doctors were able to revive her. They told us they suspected she'd had a grand mal seizure and referred us to Children's Hospital.

The doctors at Children's Hospital told us that not only had she had a grand mal seizure but she was also mentally disabled and had

Léri-Weill syndrome and some sort of bone disease. They also used the word *dwarf* in there somewhere. They said she would be lucky if she grew to be four feet tall.

We didn't care about the gloom-and-doom words they used about her disabling conditions because she was our girl. The only things that mattered to us were these seizures. And they mattered greatly because they started happening more frequently. As a result, we had to be careful to stay within a certain radius of a hospital and became frequent visitors to the emergency room.

We quickly learned what triggered her seizures. When she cried hard, she would hold her breath and not let her air out. You can imagine—every time she cried we panicked. It didn't take long for her to learn that she could get her way by crying. None of us wanted her to go into a seizure. Even so, she was soon having over five seizures a day. Hoping to stop them, the pediatric neurologist medicated her more and more until she was like a zombie.

Not wanting her to have to live in a bubble, I prayed for God to show me what to do. "Please, Lord, give me wisdom," I pleaded day after day. Then it came to me. I would teach Esther to blow on my finger. If she did that, she would have to exhale and let her air out.

Excited, I told the doctor about my plan and asked him what he thought. The look on his face said it all: *This dumb woman just fell off a turnip truck.* But what he said was a simple but firm "That won't work."

I smiled at him and didn't tell him I had already decided to try it no matter what he said. What could it hurt?

I showed Esther what I wanted her to do, and she understood right away. "Like blowing on a candle." We laughed and made a game out of it. Every so often during the day, I held up my finger and told her to blow on it. Esther was strong willed and didn't want to do it all the time I told her to. It was a tough call, but I knew there had to be consequences for her behavior when she disobeyed. This was critically important for her health and survival. And I knew she would learn to respond quickly only if I was consistent.

The next time she started to cry and hold her breath, I held up my finger and said, "Blow, Esther! Blow!" It was a struggle for her, but she did it.

I couldn't believe it! It worked! She didn't have a seizure! I screamed and yelled like a crazy woman, and my boys thought I'd lost it. I was so excited, I called Domingo, who was just as excited as I was. We both knew it was God who had given us that wisdom.

From then on, every time Esther started to cry, Domingo, our boys, or I would put up a finger and say, "Blow, Esther! Blow!" and every time she blew she didn't have a seizure.

When she hadn't had a seizure in a long time, I decided to talk to the doctor about weaning her off her medication. He was not happy, but when he heard how she was doing, he reluctantly agreed.

She started to blossom and become alive. It was amazing! It was a miracle! She was no longer lethargic. We turned to God and thanked him for revealing not only the solution but also himself to us.

I made another appointment with the doctor, knowing he was not going to be happy and might not believe me. So I asked Domingo to go with me. When the doctor came in, we told him what we had done and how well Esther was doing. He looked stern and didn't say much as we shared our story. He then stood up, excused himself, and walked out the door.

Domingo and I looked at each other, baffled. Where was he going? Was he upset? Panic swept through me as I began to fear that social services might take her away from us. Domingo looked calm and told me not to worry.

A few minutes later the doctor returned with some of his colleagues. He turned to them and said, "This is the little girl I was telling you about. She is the one *we* taught to blow on a finger so she doesn't hold her breath and trigger a seizure."

Domingo and I just looked at each other and smiled.

chapter 7

Joseph and Alfred

1987

Over the years Esther's joy and laughter transformed us despite her challenging health issues that demanded constant attention. Honestly, we didn't mind.

But her presence made us wonder how many other children were out there who needed to be loved and cared for.

When she turned five, we decided that being the center of attention probably wasn't good for her, so we thought about adopting another child. And then our pastor preached on James 1:27: "Religion that God our Father accepts as pure and faultless is this: to look after orphans and widows in their distress and to keep oneself from being polluted by the world" (NIV).

Being simple people and believing the Bible literally, we felt that through this verse God was encouraging us to pursue the adoption of more children. However, we believed that something this big needed to be a united family decision. Not only were Domingo and

I growing spiritually, but our sons were as well, so we knew we could trust their input.

We asked our sons what they thought about us adopting a little boy. They were concerned that we had our hands full with Esther's health issues and mental challenges and wouldn't be able to give another child enough attention. But they agreed we all needed to pray about it.

Within the week, both boys came to us separately and said we should pursue adopting another child. Soon our kitchen table was again covered with papers as we filled out the lengthy applications. Since God had shown us over and over that he would hold our hands and guide us through the difficulties of a special-needs child, this time we stated on our application that we would take the child with the most needs. With excitement and anticipation, the four of us began to pray for our son who we hadn't yet met.

A few months later we got a call from our social worker. She told us she had a six-year-old boy—but there was a catch. She invited us to come to her office where she could discuss the situation more easily.

I was both excited and scared. I kept reminding myself that whatever the problem, this child was God's gift and he was going to be our son.

When we arrived at the social worker's office, she seated us, then took her own seat behind her desk. She seemed a little nervous, hesitant to tell us the issue. She placed her hands on top of a file. "Well. There are *two* boys. Brothers who are currently in separate foster homes."

My breath caught. *Two! Lord,* I said silently, *we said we'd take any child, but we never said two!*

The social worker went on to tell us that the older boy, Joseph, was nine and had often been in charge of his six younger siblings because their mother would disappear for days at a time. He'd go out at night, searching for food he could steal or scrounge for his siblings.

Eventually the mother rounded up all the children and took them to the county office, where they were put in a room and given something to eat. The mother said she couldn't take care of them anymore and did not want them to go to any family members. Then she left the children without saying good-bye.

The children were split up and put into separate foster homes. Joseph went into a rage—not because his mother had left, but because he was torn from his brothers and sisters. He screamed and cried and begged. And he vowed he would find them.

As the social worker spoke, my heart broke for this little boy. His fierce spirit reminded me of the young boy who had been so determined to care for those he loved that he married his pregnant girlfriend.

Joseph hadn't found most of his siblings. But he had discovered that his six-year-old brother, Alfred, lived a couple of miles away. So at night Joseph would walk the two miles through an old farming community—which was dark and quite dangerous—to read a book to Alfred so he could go to sleep.

"You can see why we'd really like to keep these boys together." The social worker sat back in her chair and looked at us, waiting. I was so fearful that I wanted to bolt. Thoughts swirled through my mind, making it hard for me to think. As afraid as I was, how could we say no? How could we separate them? I knew what God wanted from us—obedience. And I needed to trust him. To take his hand for the difficult journey ahead.

Joseph had dark black hair and cheeks like a chipmunk; he looked a bit like Mowgli from *The Jungle Book*. He had a sly, smug smile that made me wonder what he was thinking. He held his head high and exuded so much confidence, behaving much like a grown man in a short body.

He had been staying with a wonderful foster family. They had gone out of their way to get him and his little brother together when they could. And when Domingo went to collect Joseph, he filled the truck bed with Joseph's belongings.

When we got to Alfred's foster home to pick him up, the family was eating a nice, big dinner that smelled delicious. But Alfred sat at a small table by himself, eating beans. As we left, the foster mother handed me a paper sack with Alfred's clothes—one old shirt and a pair of torn shorts. Yet I saw closets full of clothes for the other kids in the house.

Our older boys, now eighteen and sixteen, warmly welcomed their little brothers, were kind to them, and loved on them. Everything went reasonably well the first night until we put Alfred in the tub to bathe him. He began screaming and couldn't be calmed. Later we found out that his foster family had put him in a tub of hot water to punish him.

In a short time I became aware that I was in over my head. Alfred and Joseph were a handful—wild, out-of-control, rambunctious, bratty little boys.

Joseph was especially difficult for me to even consider loving. He had every bad habit I could imagine. He was so strong willed. He could—and did—stuff a double cheeseburger into his mouth in one shove. He decided he was in charge of our household and tried to run it, no matter how many times we told him we were the parents and we were in charge. At the time I didn't consider that this behavior was a sign of a lack of trust. He didn't trust that we would take care of him and his brother. After all, aside from his short time with the temporary foster family, neglect was all he'd ever known.

One day he got into trouble at school. I told him that when his dad came home he would have to tell him what he had done. It was the first time I saw Joseph struggle. The rest of the day he didn't smile, and he picked fights with the other kids. He even got mad at his brother, who he usually guarded and protected.

When Domingo got home and I called the kids to dinner, Joseph didn't come. We looked all over for him, and when we couldn't find him, we realized he had run away. I felt sick and scared. He hadn't eaten dinner, and it was so cold out. I breathed a quick prayer: "Dear God, he's just a little boy."

The police came to our home. I was scared, and my words seemed stuck in my mouth. Domingo gave the police a picture of Joseph and told them a little about him. I had expected them to judge us, but they surprised me with how kind they were.

It was dark out by the time they left. We couldn't sit still or think about anything but Joseph. Then the call finally came—they had found Joseph asleep in the neighbor's trash can.

What? I couldn't believe it. Asleep in the neighbor's trash can? What child would do that? I guess he'd had to take care of himself and survive on his own for so long that he was only doing what he'd probably done many times before.

The officer sat down with Joseph and told him he was a lucky boy to have parents who chose to adopt him. He told him there were many kids who weren't so lucky. He also told him he'd seen his room. "Why would you choose a trash can over that?" the officer asked.

Joseph's reply chiseled away a piece of the hard shell covering my heart: "I didn't want my dad to be mad at me."

After the police left, I felt like such a failure. There was so much work to do, in Joseph as well as in me. I didn't know how to handle this boy. The shame I felt was unbearable. The incident also brought to light the truth that I didn't really love him. But how could that be? Wasn't I his mom? Why didn't I have emotions for him?

When you raise a child from infancy, you have a variety of good memories from which you develop a deep emotional bond with your child. So when that child reaches a difficult life stage, you sort of have a credit in your emotional bank to draw from, enabling you to get through it. But when you adopt older children, you don't have those sweet memories that have built up a savings account of overflowing, unconditional love. You have only negative behavior that needs constant attention and correction.

I got so discouraged by the way I felt toward Joseph that I often got on my knees and cried to God to help me love this child. I even called my husband at work, crying and in deep despair—"I'm such a failure as a mom to Joseph. I feel terrible."

Domingo said, "Irene, you *are* loving him. You are serving him, meeting his needs, and most of all you are sacrificially doing all you can to teach and train him. That is agape love, the love God requires of you. After a while the emotion will come."

I knew this was true because God had showed me this in my marriage to Domingo. I had gone from hate to love and respect. The only way I could see to get through this was to love Joseph with Christ's love. To persevere.

I hung up, taking Domingo's words to heart, and decided to wait on God. Even so, it was no easy task. I had to frequently remind myself that Joseph was the boy who had run away because he had gotten into trouble at school. He was the crazy kid who had slept in a trash can. That Alfred was the little boy abandoned by his mother, separated from his siblings, and scalded as a form of punishment.

The boys adjusted to our home and schedule quickly. I give a lot of credit to our sons Vincent and Anthony for that. They loved their little brothers and showed them the ropes, encouraging them and guiding them to the right thing when they did something wrong.

Alfred had a smile that stretched from ear to ear. He was like a Mexican jumping bean. Always moving, jumping, and running—most of the time away from me. He would steal, then look at me with bright eyes and say, "Never saw it, never touched it." Then later we'd find the object in his pocket. He was like one of the Little Rascals—filled with so much mischief. When thinking about him, I could only use the word *híjole* to describe him. It's a Spanish word loosely translated, "Is this for real? Holy guacamole!"

Alfred and Esther were the same age and got along really well. They got into a lot of mischief together, and as most siblings do, they'd get into scuffles as well. As tiny as Esther was, she stood her ground. Soon Alfred knew how far he could push her, and he'd go right to the edge of that line.

It was great to see Esther's social skills progressing now that she had a sibling her age. Even if fighting was a part of that progress.

Alfred followed Joseph everywhere and did whatever Joseph asked him to do. He was like Joseph's personal slave, and Joseph loved it. He liked to parent Alfred. After all, he was used to being "dad" to all his siblings.

Eventually Alfred started to make up his own mind about things and started telling his brother no. This infuriated Joseph. He didn't want to release Alfred to us and let us parent him. He wanted all the control over his brother. Yet as hard as he was on Alfred, it warmed my heart to see how soft he was with Esther. He protected her like a guard dog and even rebuked Alfred if he so much as looked at her cross-eyed.

chapter 8

Marie, Felix, and Doreen

For twenty-four years Domingo had worked for his brother-in-law in the automotive shop and was the corporate vice president. But ever since he quit drinking and going to the races, things had changed. He was no longer part of the inside jokes, the socializing after work. After his alcoholic sister's death from cirrhosis of the liver, things were different between him and his brother-in-law. Domingo was seeing more situations where he was being asked to do things against his convictions. He had made a promise to obey God and not man, so he knew he couldn't stay. He had been promised many benefits as a long-term employee, but he walked away from it all to stand by his convictions.

A few months later he started his own automotive and machine shop. It was small, but it was ours. The good news was that it was doing well. The bad news was that Domingo was working day and night again, leaving me to care for the five children by myself. These two young boys especially needed to spend time with their dad, but it wasn't possible.

A year passed, and the boys were settling in a little more all the time. They certainly were not easy, but God was faithful to give us the strength and endurance we needed. They had so many bad habits but were making forward progress in small steps. Both boys loved sports, and each had one in which he excelled. For Joseph, it was soccer. He was like a prima ballerina on the soccer field, able to manipulate the ball from foot to foot and kick it precisely where he wanted it to go. I'd never seen such a young boy control a ball with so much grace and finesse. It was so beautiful to watch, it took my breath away. He was a natural, and many coaches in the community wanted him on their teams. He eventually made the elite club soccer team—the one he'd hoped to join. We were all so excited for him and proud of him.

Alfred, on the other hand, excelled at gymnastics, especially the floor exercise. This was no surprise, considering he was my little Mexican jumping bean. Now instead of jumping up and down, he was doing backflips everywhere. He was this goofy little kid who loved to be in the air instead of on the ground.

Life was busy, but I didn't mind. I knew we were doing God's work, and that's all that mattered to me.

Then I received a call at work from Joseph's former social worker. "Irene," he said, "I have an emergency. We have a twelve-year-old girl who was molested in her foster home and needs to leave right away. She has a fourteen-year-old brother who also needs to be placed."

I couldn't believe he was dumping this on me while I was at work. What I wanted to say was "Are you kidding me? Why don't you call someone else?" Instead, I said with a calmness I didn't feel, "I'll talk it over with Domingo and get back to you."

"I need to know right away. So if you can call me before night-time, I'd appreciate it."

I hung up, already knowing what my answer was going to be. Who would take a twelve-year-old girl and a fourteen-year-old boy? Only crazy people. And we weren't *that* crazy.

I asked my assistant to rinse my client's hair while I called Domingo. My knees shook, and my stomach went sour. I didn't want any more kids. "Why us, Mingo? Our hands are full. Can't they call someone else?"

Domingo answered in his calm, confident way with a question of his own. "What do you think God wants us to do?"

So many times we are at a crossroads in life. We can choose the easy path and miss out on God's blessings. Or we can take the hard path, knowing that Jesus is leading the way. My first thought, my strongest desire, was to choose the easy path. I had three adopted kids. I was doing enough—more than most people I knew. I wanted to argue with Domingo. To remind him how difficult our life already was. How adding two more kids with great needs would pull us under.

"Irene, these kids need a family."

It was as though someone had thrown ice water on me, and I came to my senses. I knew the right thing to do. I knew without a doubt what God was asking. I called the social worker and told him our decision.

As I cut my client's hair, her voice faded to the background as I became absorbed in my own conflicting thoughts. Many Christians, rather than spurring us on to care for the orphans, had told us not to take in any more children. I was amazed and saddened that I was more concerned about what people would think of me than about the task God had given me to do.

But how could we say no to God? We didn't need a divine revelation about whether to take in these siblings; we already knew God's will through James 1:27. The verse didn't tell us to take in only a certain number of orphans. Or to pray about whether we had enough resources. The verse said to care for them. Period. Our prayers were for God to give us the courage to obey his word. We asked him to hold our hands and take us through this journey ahead.

When the kids arrived later that day, my heart broke. The girl, Marie, seemed to shrink into herself. She was dressed sloppily and all in black, keeping her head so low her hair hid her face. When I got her to look me in the eyes, I could see how pretty she was. I wanted to hold her and love on her, but there was a coolness about her that made me keep my distance. She seemed so compliant and beaten down. I knew this young girl had suffered her share of hardships, but she obviously had such a sweet spirit that I knew I could eventually win her over. She needed to be loved with a real love. All she'd known was a "love" from her birth mom who preferred drugs to her daughter.

Her brother, Felix, on the other hand, strutted up to the front door as though he was somebody important with his own entourage trailing along behind. He looked through the door, checking everything out, as though deciding whether this house was good enough for him to set foot in. Then he walked right past me as though I was invisible and said to no one in particular, "Where's my room?"

I moved to stand in front of him. "In my home you will need to acknowledge me."

His chin tipped up and he said, "I don't have to do anything I don't want to. I have a lawyer, and I have rights."

My blood curdled. I wanted to get in his face and scream at him, "Get out now!" Thankfully, the Spirit controlled my anger. Instead, I said, "That's fine. You can take your rights, your lawyer, and yourself right out of our home. In this house I have the right to ask you to leave."

He backed down, defiance still written all over his face.

Joseph and the other kids watched from a distance. Alfred and Esther were excited and anxious to meet them. Joseph, watching every move the older boy made, became very protective of me.

Once I showed Felix to the room he would share with Joseph, I retreated to my room and closed the door behind me, fearful, trembling, and crying.

Within a few days of dealing with the new kids, I became aware of how far Joseph and Alfred had come. Joseph was learning to trust us and relinquish his role as the one in charge. He was enjoying being a normal kid.

A few months later, Marie and I were in the car together, listening to Christian talk radio. The topic? "Staying Pure for Your Mate."

Marie began to squirm, her brows drawing together. "Do you think God loves girls who aren't pure?"

Her point-blank question surprised me. She had been so closed that I didn't expect such an open question. I wanted to cry. This girl had been sexually assaulted and used, feeling guilt that didn't belong to her but to those who had stolen her innocence and purity.

I pulled the car over, then said a quick prayer in my head as I turned off the engine. I began to gently share with her that God loves us even when we aren't pure. I explained that with the gift of salvation, Jesus makes us all pure again.

Together we prayed, and she asked him to forgive her of all she had done and to be the one who guided her life.

After the amen, she began to share her past with me. I'd known very little, but now I knew the larger story. No child should have to endure all she did—and all because her birth mom was an addict who used her children to help her get drugs.

Marie and Felix had been with us about a year when the social worker contacted us to say that their nine-year-old sister, Doreen, needed a home. The social worker was unusually honest and straight-forward about Doreen's issues. Since most social workers downplayed the issues of the children they were trying to place, when she told us Doreen was wild, rebellious, and mean, we knew she was really, really bad.

There were so many reasons to say no. We were knee-deep in muck already. Domingo was still working long hours. I was doing most of the childcare for six children alone. And yet my heart reached out to this little girl.

What was I thinking? Did I think we could save the world one child at a time?

When we brought it up to the family, Felix and Marie begged us to take in their little sister. Felix tried to convince us to take her by offering to help us in any way he could to teach her the rules of our home. He seemed confident that she would listen to him and that he would be able to influence her. Now this was a boy who was very self-centered, so this really touched my heart. Sadly, we would soon learn that this little wild child listened to no one—not even Felix!

By now Felix was doing pretty well—better than we had expected. He still had a mouth on him, but at least he was trying, and I didn't want to mess that up by bringing in his difficult sister.

But once again, how could we say no to God? The house we lived in was God's home. Shouldn't it be filled with orphans?

Before climbing into bed that night, Domingo and I prayed, but this time my prayers were different—"Lord, please take away my fear. Forgive me for the doubts in my heart. Show me your way, O Lord."

And then Domingo prayed. "Thank you, Lord, for the opportunity to serve you. Spend us until we are totally dependent on you. Bring us the trials that perfect us and draw us nearer to you." (Oh, how my husband had been transformed, becoming my spiritual leader and an example not only to me but to many.)

As I waited for sleep to come, I thought about the apostles. What had they thought when Jesus said, "Follow me," asking them to leave everything they'd known? Later, when they really understood what they'd said yes to, had they felt it was unfair that their lives had changed so dramatically in one day? Had they ever resented that no one else was asked to give up all they had?

For Domingo and me, ever since we had become Christians—truly wanting to make Jesus the Lord of our lives—our lives were continually changing. At times the pace was so fast it was hard to keep up. During those seasons I would get on my knees and plead with God, "Fill me up, Lord, so that I have the ability to do your will."

The words in Isaiah 40:30–31 came to me, bringing comfort and hope: "Even youths will become weak and tired, and young men will fall in exhaustion. But those who trust in the LORD will find new strength. They will soar high on wings like eagles. They will run and not grow weary. They will walk and not faint."

Doreen

The day came for Doreen to arrive. My stomach churned as I waited. I knew this would be tough for our family. It seemed that just as we were settling in with one set of kids, more would come and upset the relative calm place we'd reached.

Despite what the social worker had told us, I wondered if Doreen would have a sweet spirit like her sister. Her foster mother had told me she liked to dress and act like a boy, and so she treated Doreen like one.

Marie shared with me that Doreen had lived in a bad environment with her birth dad, who was a heroin addict. I knew that out of such an environment there were sure to be many disturbing stories, but I believed that with God's wisdom and help we would get through the obstacles that we'd encounter.

Doreen was a beautiful girl. Her eyes sparkled with an amazing green and yellow color. When the social worker introduced us, Doreen looked me straight in the eyes, clearly displaying not a confident respect, but rather defiance and a very strong will. I was taken aback somewhat and felt a shudder run through me.

As her foster mother had warned, Doreen was dressed like a boy. When she came in the house, she could see through the back window that the other kids were swimming. In a flash she stripped off her top, kicked off her high-tops, ran outside, and jumped into the pool.

Time stopped. Everyone was in shock, including the kids in the pool. I was not only stunned but mortified as well. I unfroze myself and dashed out the door. I couldn't catch my breath quickly enough to tell her to get some clothes on.

It was then I understood that this beautiful, wild creature really thought she was a boy.

For school I bought her clothes more suitable for a girl. She left the house looking cute, got to school, and immediately slipped into the bathroom to change into the boy clothes she had brought with her to our home—Levi's, Nike high-tops, and T-shirts.

One day the principal called and asked me to come to the school right away. When I got there, Doreen was sitting in his office, the defiant look confidently on her face, her arms crossed against her T-shirt-clad chest. Her teacher sat in another chair, looking beat.

The principal pointed to the only vacant chair in the small room. "Please have a seat, Mrs. Garcia."

I knew by the look on the principal's face that this was not going to be a pleasant meeting. He leaned forward, took a deep breath, and said, "Doreen is going to be expelled for her actions, so we need to discuss which school you would like her transferred to. She is nothing but trouble, and I don't want her in my school anymore."

I knew this girl was no angel, but I had no idea what she'd done to deserve expulsion and told the principal so.

He proceeded to give me a list of offenses, ticking them off on his fingers. "She mouths off to her teacher and leaves the classroom without permission. The teacher cannot handle her. This isn't the first time. It happens frequently. Today she beat up a boy for calling her a girl. That's the last straw. The other kids are afraid of her."

I stared at him, astounded and angry. "How long has this been going on? Why wasn't I told any of this before?"

It was the principal's turn to look astounded and confused. "You didn't know Doreen was walking out of the class and being defiant?"

"This is the first time I've heard anything about this." I turned to look at the teacher. "Why didn't you notify me about her behavior?"

"Well," she said, looking indignant, "I sent a note home with Doreen."

I looked at her, thankful she couldn't read my mental response: *Are you really that stupid?* Instead, I took a deep breath, struggling to keep calm. "Was I supposed to reply?"

The woman just looked at me.

"Did you really think a child like Doreen would even give me the note?" I turned to the principal. "Can we meet privately?"

The teacher was dismissed, and Doreen was sent to sit outside the office.

Once they were gone, I spoke my mind. "I don't think it's fair to expel Doreen for all these offenses when I wasn't made aware of them and given the chance to deal with them."

"What do you suggest?"

As we talked, we came up with a solution: I would come to class with Doreen every day and sit in the back of the classroom until she learned to behave. I would also sit with her during lunch, which would embarrass her to no end. I hoped that would be motivation enough for her to begin straightening up.

I drove home with Doreen in the backseat, feeling that Domingo and I were in over our heads. Again. My hope was that I had the same Holy Spirit Jesus had when he endured the cross. It helped to keep this in perspective—the difficulties Doreen brought to our family were nothing compared to what Jesus faced on the cross.

Doreen was one of the hardest girls I have ever raised. No one could tame this wild child. She demanded attention, and if she didn't get it, she'd do whatever she could to make that happen. I really wanted to help her, but she did not listen to me or Domingo. The limitations set on us by the foster care system stipulated that time-out was the only acceptable disciplinary measure. A lot of good that did. When we put her in time-out, she'd look at us and laugh. I felt as though nothing was going to change her hard and defiant heart. Doreen had been abused by her father, who she loved dearly. She felt that men had more power, and she wanted to be one and hurt those who were weaker.

Whenever she did cruel things at school, the tough kids celebrated her acts and the good kids stayed away, reinforcing her bad behavior. Being cool and the center of attention was her strongest motivation. So we made the decision to take her out of public school, and I began to homeschool her, along with the other kids.

I was not an avid homeschooling mom and didn't homeschool my kids because I wanted to; I did it because I felt I had no choice. I couldn't be at school all the time and give the other kids as much attention as they needed as well. Besides, all these kids seemed to gravitate toward other rebellious and lost souls in the public school. Homeschooling was a way to give our kids the special attention they needed.

But taking Doreen out of public school didn't help her meanness at all. She was a very dark little girl, capable of hurting other children. She had a foul mouth and wounded others deeply with her words. She fought with all her other siblings, being as mean as could be to them—except Joseph. Doreen looked up to him and wanted to play sports the way he did.

I became so distraught that nothing seemed to get through to her. I went into my bathroom and got on my knees and prayed, "Lord, do whatever it takes to change this girl's heart."

My one hope was that the legal guardian process, which had taken nearly a year, was almost complete. I thought perhaps that would be the turning point for her—she would be ours.

chapter 9

storm clouds

One summer, I had the opportunity to take Doreen and Esther for a week to a Christian summer camp called Forest Home. The kids slept on cots in tepees and ate outside and learned all about God's love. Neither girl had ever been to camp, and both wanted to go. Although I'd never left the other kids to go anywhere for an extended period of time, I felt this would be a good opportunity for the girls, so I went as the counselor for a group of seven campers from our church, including my two girls. I knew I needed to go to protect Esther from the other kids and the other kids from Doreen.

The day we left was my birthday. The family came to the church to send us off on the bus that would take us up the mountain to camp. I gave everyone a hug and a kiss good-bye. When Domingo, whose back had recently gone out, reached for my bag, Joseph stopped him. "I'll carry it, Dad." Joseph walked me to the bus, my bag in one hand.

I was so proud of him. Oh, how I'd learned to love this animated and charismatic child. Domingo's words suddenly echoed in my mind. He had been right. The act of loving Joseph with God's agape love had turned into a flooding emotion. This was my boy, and I loved him with all my heart.

At the bus, I grabbed his face and kissed it all over. He chuckled and smiled his beautiful smile that made me feel limp. "Joseph," I said, "I feel as though you are flesh of my flesh. You bring me such joy. I'm proud to be called your mom."

His grin grew even wider, and he threw his arms around me.

"Good-bye, Son."

"Good-bye, Mom."

I stepped onto the bus, realizing that I'd gone from not liking this kid much at all to feeling as though my heart would burst with all the love I had for him. As I sat on the bus, squirming kids opening and closing the windows, the warm winds flowing through, I felt somewhat like Mary—pondering all these things of God in my heart. How God could change a heart so selfish that I couldn't love a bratty kid to where, four years later, I loved him to overflowing. How God could take an angry, rebellious boy and create a complete turnaround.

When I got to camp and opened my suitcase to unpack, I found a stuffed monkey with a note attached. Joseph had tucked it inside when I wasn't looking. I held the monkey as I read the sweet note he'd given me, wishing me a happy birthday, telling me how much he loved me, and thanking me for his new life. I couldn't have asked for a greater birthday gift.

We had a wonderful week, singing camp songs, swimming, hiking, playing camp games, and being together, focusing on God and one another. I kept in touch with the family by using the pay phone in the center of the main camp each afternoon. The kids at home were not doing well with one of us gone. They were defiant and mouthy. Not all that surprising with all those teens and preteens.

On Friday, a strange feeling nagged me all day. I felt anxious enough that I went into the main camp early to call Domingo at work. He relayed that the babysitter was having a difficult time with the children—especially Joseph. I was so upset that when we hung up, I dialed our home number, ready to let Joseph have it. As the phone rang, I decided I'd rather deal with him face-to-face when I got home the next day. This was so unlike me. I preferred to deal with issues immediately.

That night after we'd fallen asleep, a counselor came for me, saying Domingo was on the phone. I knew something serious had happened, since Domingo would never call in the middle of the night. As we drove down the hill, I ran all kinds of possibilities through my mind. I thought Domingo must be hurt since he could already barely move before I left. I prayed God would give me the strength to receive the news.

But as we came into camp, I saw my husband and my two oldest boys waiting for me. I don't know why, but I knew immediately what had happened. I pulled my sweater around me as if I could warm myself from the chilling news.

"There's been an accident, Irene," Domingo said, and he started to cry. "I found Joseph in his closet. On his knees. Strangled with a belt around his neck." He took a breath. "I got him down and gave him CPR. But his eyes wouldn't open. He wouldn't breathe." More tears came, and the pain in Domingo's eyes cut straight through me. I couldn't bear it. "It made no sense, Irene. All he had to do was stand up. Why didn't he stand up? What was he thinking?"

I don't even know if I can describe how I felt. This wonderful boy who had stolen my heart was gone—forever. I would never see his smile or hear his voice again. Despair took control of me. There was nothing I could do to change what had happened. My heart ached, my head spun, my legs felt like they were not connected, and this uncontrollable heart-wrenched sobbing took control of every part of my being as I leaned into Domingo and he put his arms around me, his sobs mingling with mine.

On our way down the mountain, I thought of the call I had made earlier in the day. If I'd yelled at Joseph on the phone, my words and the tone I would have used could have tormented me the rest of my life.

When I got home, I went into his room, looking for something to help me understand what had happened. I was so confused. What had he been doing in the closet? Had it been an accident? Or had he purposefully taken his life? He was such a prankster that I wondered if he had been trying to play a joke on his siblings. The investigators said it had to have been an accident because even a grown man wouldn't be able to stay on his knees to suffocate himself. The body's natural tendency is to get air, so any person in that situation would automatically stand up when the air supply is cut off. The investigator thought Joseph was fooling around and somehow passed out. His head fell forward over the belt, constricting his airway, and he suffocated.

I searched his room and found a note in a pocket in a pair of pants that said, "I want to be a better Christian and be more like Jesus."

Although that didn't answer my question about what had happened, at least God gave me the hope I needed—to know I would see my precious boy again in heaven.

God used Joseph to touch many lives. Some came to know the Lord at his memorial service.

There weren't enough arms to hold the hurting surviving children. Friends stepped up to each take a child, but Doreen refused to be held. She didn't even want to be touched. And yet she cried. It was the first time I'd ever seen her cry. Her crying revealed the brokenness in her—she was mentally and spiritually defeated. Her wall of defiance came crashing down.

Domingo and I had to put our grief on hold so we could take on the pain of our wounded children. It was so much to bear, I often thought I wasn't going to make it. But, as always, Domingo was our pillar of strength.

That day changed us all forever; in a way, Joseph's death killed the entire family. The crazy way he died played havoc with our minds and emotions. Some would be haunted for years by grief, and others held guilt inside them that would keep them running for decades. Many of us felt blame—if only we could have done something to prevent it.

Marie blamed herself because she'd been mean to Joseph all week. She eventually ran away, back to her birth family, where she began to take drugs with them to numb her pain.

Alfred said it was his fault because he'd fought with Joseph right before he died. He changed and became hard, then rebelled like he was mad at us.

Felix did okay for a while, then he slipped when he turned eighteen. After he graduated, he left to live with his birth family, got on meth, and was immediately addicted.

Doreen's world stopped. With Joseph no longer there to laugh and play with, she felt alone. Her best friend was gone forever.

Joseph's life was short but hard. God was so sweet to me in my grief, but my heart was still burdened with a deep ache because I had not been able to say good-bye to my son. Once when my daughter-in-law came to visit, I shared the sadness I felt. I hadn't been with Joseph when he needed me the most. I didn't get to say good-bye to my boy. It was then my daughter-in-law said, "Mom, you were the only one who got to say good-bye."

The truth of her words sank in and brought a soothing calm through me. She was right—I did get to say good-bye. As I hugged Joseph before climbing the steps into the bus and told him how much I loved him, I had said good-bye. The last words my boy heard from me were about how much he was loved and cherished by his mama.

Oh, how different it would have been if I had spoken to him in anger that day he died.

I hate that Joseph died. I hate that I had only a few short years with this boy I loved so deeply. And yet I'm so grateful that God gave us Joseph to teach me how to love. I thought I was compassionate, forgiving, and loving. And then God brought Joseph along to reveal to me who I really was—that my love doesn't cut it. I said I wanted to help orphans, but what I didn't know was how hard it would be to love them. It's always been easy for me to love the lovely ... but hard to love the unlovely. How I love others is what speaks to others about my relationship with God. First Corinthians 13:2–3 says that if I don't have love, what good are any of my works, faith, and knowledge? It says that all of this profits me nothing if there is no love. God is love, and I need to show his love to the world. What better way to show Christ's love than by taking in the unlovely—and learning to love them? Perhaps the world will see Christ in me.

Because of Joseph I know God can give me many different kinds of children and I will be able to love them all. I know that when a child comes to our home, things will be difficult at first. But my job is to be obedient to God and love through action and leave the rest to him. It doesn't mean I don't get discouraged—I do! But I know I will get through it.

Through Joseph I learned love is a choice. That truth has been proved to me many times through the years. Since that time I have learned to love many children. Through the one who created love, my love is supernatural—and it overflows. I have the power in the Spirit to love unconditionally the way I am loved. First Peter 1:22 says, "Now that you have purified yourselves by obeying the truth so that you have sincere love for each other, love one another deeply, from the heart" (NIV). Without the Spirit I couldn't love this way. Besides, God had already taught me to love and forgive Domingo. And Joseph was the next step in the teaching process.

I can love anyone—through the power of God.

chapter 10

the dark years

Doreen was completely broken by Joseph's death. Not only did she realize his death was final and there was nothing she could do about it, but I believed it also scared her. She had thought she was invincible; now she knew she wasn't.

After the funeral I asked her if she was ready to give her life to God. Through her tears she said yes. As we prayed, she asked God to forgive her of her sins. It was like a blanket of all her sins came down from heaven; she kept confessing one sin after another. She was washed clean, as white as snow.

From that day forward, Doreen did pretty well, considering who she had been before. She got involved in the youth group, made friends, and managed not to get into trouble. She would come into my room and talk to me for hours. We had many tender moments. She was a sweet girl, really. She told me she loved me, and she worried about me when the older kids started to run away.

She lived with us another ten years—until she was about twenty-one. Then she started drinking and taking drugs. She threw parties in our home when we were gone. When she got caught, instead of admitting she was wrong, she told people horrible lies about us. Once, she came to me privately to apologize. But it seemed she could never forgive herself, and she disappeared from our lives. I know she loved us. She just got caught in an ugly web of drugs and drinking. And then she went to jail.

You know the saying "It ain't over till the fat lady sings"? It's a weird analogy, but I believe there's still hope for her. God is teaching me that I have to keep praying and leave the rest up to him. When I think about Doreen, I choose to think good thoughts and replay sweet memories. I pray she will know I have forgiven her. I know there are still many unanswered prayers, and Doreen is one of them.

Vivian

About a year after Joseph's funeral, the social worker called with another plea. Would we take in Marie, Felix, and Doreen's sixteen-year-old sister, Vivian?

We felt this was what God wanted from us, and we didn't want to say no to God, even though there were times I certainly felt like it. But God wants our all, and he was asking us to give up our comforts. We had a choice, but we wanted to take the path that led toward a deeper walk with God, not one that led away from him.

Vivian wanted to be with her sister Marie. For about five years she'd lived with a wonderful, staunch Catholic woman who took her in, helped her, and taught her good morals. Then Vivian started to rebel, and the woman could no longer care for her. For some reason, Vivian did well with us. She was really easy compared to many of the others. She was small and had rosy cheeks. A darling girl, sweet and compliant.

One day I got mad at her—which was unusual—and she cried at the dinner table for a long time. I felt really bad, but I didn't think my words should have affected her that way. I had only corrected her. Later I discovered she was in turmoil and beginning to make poor choices that were pulling on her.

One of the popular Christian boys from our church was crazy about her, and she liked him, too. Then she got a job at a restaurant, met a cook in the kitchen, and liked him even more. We didn't know about him, nor about the lies she told in order to sneak around with him. Sadly, she continued to lead the Christian boy on while involved with the cook.

One day she went to visit her birth family and didn't come back. We drove up the coast to retrieve her from the police department. She told us she would rather go to juvenile hall than come home with us. It felt like a cold wind had come in and slapped both Domingo and me. We were shocked. How could her heart change so quickly? Why did she hate us? It took us both a long time to recover. We loved this girl. She had lived with us for almost two years, and most of that time was a joy, so the end was agonizing. We had to learn the hard way that these kids wouldn't always be thankful for what we did for them.

Four years after Joseph's death, at the end of 1993, Domingo decided I needed a break. He knew I was crumbling on the inside and needed some relaxation and refreshment with my mentor; so he arranged to send me to Hawaii for two weeks at the beginning of 1994 to visit with Mary Barshaw, who had moved there with her husband.

Hawaii held more than just beauty. Something in the air wrapped around me and brought peace, calm, and a sense of love. Mary and I looked forward to nice, lazy, quiet times on the beach and many deep conversations. But my dreams for a sweet vacation didn't last long. The day after I got there, on January 17, 1994, the Northridge earthquake hit California. Our house was damaged enough that the family had to move into our motor home for a week. Since flights were delayed or canceled, I couldn't get home, so Domingo had to take care of everything by himself. The kids were constantly crying, the aftershocks sending them back into fear. He couldn't buy gas, and the markets were running out of food. There was no power, which made things even more difficult.

Domingo had set up our motor home as the neighborhood command center where everyone could cook and watch the news. Neighbors helped by siphoning gas to put into the motor home.

In the past, we had never taken out earthquake insurance on our homes. For some reason, the day before I left for Hawaii, I asked our agent to add earthquake insurance to our policy. I believe God put it on my heart to take care of us.

During my week in Hawaii, Mary encouraged me as she always had, helping me get back on track spiritually. I told her I felt embarrassed by all the trials in my life, and she reminded me that being a Christian isn't easy. She had me read 1 Peter 4:12–16, which says in part, "Dear friends, don't be surprised at the fiery trials you are going through, as if something strange were happening to you. Instead, be very glad—for these trials make you partners with Christ in his suffering.... It is no shame to suffer for being a Christian."

Trials, she reminded me, were to perfect me so I could be a partner with Christ. As I talked it through with her, I began to rejoice in my trials. I had thought God was ashamed of me and that's why all these difficult things were happening.

Not long after I returned home, while the house was being repaired, Domingo's mother began doing odd things and clearly needed more help. When she was diagnosed with Alzheimer's, we moved her in with us so she could be cared for by family rather than go to a convalescent home.

It was a great heartache for us all. I loved my mother-in-law very much and admired her strength and inner beauty. She had endured so much pain and suffering in her life. But as the disease took over, she became another person. At first confused and sad, then mad and angry—a common occurrence in Alzheimer's patients. It was hard for her to understand that we were not her enemy, and it was hard for our family to see this good woman do things that were not a part of her normal character. But we knew it was right to care for her, and Domingo wanted to honor his mother in this way. I must say, it was incredibly difficult to try to care for her as well as all these kids who had behavioral issues and needed constant attention. I was driven to my knees again and again, relying completely on God for help.

My mother-in-law eventually became bedridden, and we watched her wither away until the day she took her last breath. I will never forget Domingo carrying his frail mother in his arms down the stairs, with tears rolling down his cheeks, then placing her body on a gurney.

Difficult things escalated at home. Sin is an ugly thing; it is like cancer—it keeps spreading. Marie ran away and went back to her birth family. Her returning to her destructive, drug-addicted family felt like a knife in my heart. After all we had done, how could she turn her back on us and not want to come home? How could God let this happen? "Lord, where are you?" I cried. "Please bring her back." And she did come back—addicted to meth. She left again. And again. Until we finally had to tell her not to come back.

Doreen was drinking and taking drugs. Then Esther started making really bad choices.

Alfred struggled. He tried to find his *real* parents, thinking they'd be delighted to see him. Only when he did find out about them, he discovered the horrific ugliness of his family.

During those ten dark years we dealt with Joseph's death, a woman who had Alzheimer's, daughters who had been molested, pregnancies, drugs, children running away, children stealing, sexual promiscuity, rebellion, lying, and drinking. I had given everything I had to my family, never holding back. I loved them all so much and wanted the best for them. But with all this, I felt like I was a failure as a mom. I was ashamed and still felt as though I had disappointed God.

I must confess, when I first chose to be a foster parent of children with difficult emotional pasts, I really believed that if I loved them, they would love me back. They would be thankful to us for taking them in, everything would work out nicely, and we would all have happy endings. Our kids would have grand transformations, follow God, and be forever thankful to us for caring for them through their difficult years.

Boy, was I wrong. And what selfish thinking on my part! Better yet, what prideful thinking.

I know at times I was the one who made a mess out of things, but I did the best I could. I can't tell you the number of tears I shed throughout those years. I now have bad knees, and I believe it's because I was on them so much, pleading with God to help me get through the trials.

People didn't understand. They said, "These aren't your kids; let them go." It broke my heart. When God adopted me, it was permanent. No matter how much I rebelled, God never let me go. In the same way, when we adopted our children, it was permanent. God never says, "Because you sinned, I am no longer your Father." When Domingo and I adopt our children, they know they will always be loved and always be ours. Even though some are still caught in the consequences of their choices, they are still our kids. They always will be.

I collapsed under the weight of it all. I told Domingo I wanted to leave him. I wanted out. I was done. I told people to never foster; the heartache was too great. I yelled at God to leave me alone. I'd had enough from him.

That was the lowest point of my life.

It didn't take long before I was begging God to forgive me for what I'd said and thought. I was so ashamed. When I shared my despair and exhaustion with a friend, she reminded me that I'd been praying to be poured out until there was nothing left. How could I be angry? My God was answering my prayers. He hadn't forsaken me. He was right next to me.

I must confess, I am a little more careful what I pray for now.

Esther grows up

Esther became a teenager during the dark years. And even though she brought lots of joy to our family, we also faced many heartaches and disappointments. The hardest were her teen years, when she wanted to be like all the other girls. She did so many dumb and childish things that girls her age didn't want to be around her. I could understand their reluctance. She wanted so badly to be a part of a group of girls her age that she made up things so the girls would accept her, not realizing they all knew she wasn't telling the truth. They could also be cruel without realizing it.

We wanted to protect her from the unintentional cruelty of the girls her age, but we couldn't. As a result, she started to gravitate toward kids who accepted her—kids who were making poor choices.

These things hurt Domingo and me so much, but we knew the only thing we could do was help her get through those years.

Near the end of the dark years, I decided to pursue my first love—teaching. I loved dissecting God's Word and teaching young women how to be godly in all areas of their lives. I wanted to teach them how to love their future husbands. I wanted to write Bible study material. So I began to teach and mentor college girls. It was so exciting to see the understanding in their faces when they really *got it*.

However, I noticed that most of them surprisingly didn't know the first thing about cooking, cleaning, or entertaining. Since Esther was little, she had worked in the kitchen with me—and loved it. She was always there setting the table, cleaning up. She developed her own delicious recipes. She helped keep the house clean, and again, she liked doing it. Once she was old enough to drive, she'd go to the store to buy groceries for me. However, I knew that, due to her disabilities, she wouldn't be able to go to college and get a great job. I wondered what she'd do for a career when she could only help run a household.

And then it hit me. Here I'd been teaching young women about a woman's role, yet I'd missed this truth for Esther. Nowhere in the Bible does it say, "Older women teach the young girls to go to college and become academic and intellectual." No, it says, "Older women likewise are to be reverent in their behavior, not malicious gossips nor enslaved to much wine, teaching what is good, so that they may encourage the young women to love their husbands, to love their children, to be sensible, pure, workers at home, kind, being subject to their own husbands, so that the word of God will not be dishonored" (Titus 2:3–5 NASB).

Duh, I thought. How foolish I was. I had been unable to see beyond what I knew, focusing on what the world expected out of a young woman. My job was to teach my daughter godly principles and the role of a woman. In my desire for her to be like all the other girls, I'd lost sight of what God had called me to teach *her*. God would take it from there. And he has.

Esther has been the biggest blessing for Domingo and me. It's because of her gifts of service and hospitality that we have been able to care for our ten children who live at home now. She helps me by cooking, cleaning, grocery shopping, and driving the kids around. She often invites guests to our home and helps prepare the meals for them.

She was a part of God's plan for this family from the beginning. And this family was part of God's plan for her from the beginning.

Ephesians 2:10 says, "For we are His workmanship, created in Christ Jesus for good works, which God prepared beforehand so that we would walk in them" (NASB). God created Esther for a purpose and for his good works. I just thought I had to figure that out for her. But I had to stop worrying about her future and believe that she was God's child, created for God's good works. Like all of us, she didn't have to be intellectual; she just had to be obedient.

baby George

Marie got in contact with us again and then came home. She had just started to do well when she met up with an old friend. For six weeks they got high on cocaine, and she ended up pregnant. I was so ashamed of what she had done until I remembered being fifteen and pregnant. I understood how my mom must have felt.

Marie came home, and we told her we would help her and take care of her during her pregnancy. However, I held tight to my feelings, determined not to let her hurt me again. When she had started running away, I wanted to die because the pain was so tormenting. I felt so roughed up inside. Nothing soothed my wounds. For a while I even stopped praying—I was so bitter and resentful toward God. Her continual running away and coming back had so deeply hurt and wounded me that I didn't want to give my heart out again.

The day Marie went into labor, Esther was scheduled for surgery. Domingo felt he should be with Esther and I should go with Marie. My daughter-in-law was her birthing coach, so I could go in and out of her room to see how she was doing. Honestly, it was so difficult for me to be with Marie. That day I really struggled with my emotions.

I loved Marie, but I really felt I needed to keep my distance from her and the baby, to hold on tightly to my heart because it could so easily break. I knew that if I let my guard down, I would fall madly in love with her baby.

At one point as I started walking out of the room, the doctor said, "The baby is coming any minute. Aren't you going to stay?"

What could I do? I wanted to run but felt too embarrassed to leave, so I did what most moms do—I sat and waited. As I sat there, watching my daughter give birth, I felt a deep sadness. Don't misunderstand me—I was happy that this baby was being born, but I knew he would have so many obstacles in his life. As I sat in the room, the only thing I could think of was that I was going to end up being the one responsible for this child. That was the last thing I wanted. I didn't want another child. I had three teenagers who were using drugs. I was so worn-out. I was done raising someone else's kids. I had nothing to give; I was on empty.

But Domingo had reminded me that Marie could've chosen to have an abortion; instead she chose life. That stopped me in my tracks. He was right. An abortion would've been easier for her; no one would've ever known. I was eternally grateful she chose life, so for that I praised God.

Now I was sitting in a hospital room, waiting to see life in its beginning stages, praying all would be well for this child as he entered this world.

All of a sudden the labor room turned into a delivery room, and I was overwhelmed by the elegance and tenderness of a mother giving birth. Then this fascinating little creature appeared—and in an instant my soft feelings were again hardened with fear. I felt a cold rush go through my body as I noticed that the baby was blue. *Oh God, he's not crying!* The look of alarm on the faces around us brought a strong sense of panic over me. I started praying as I watched the doctor and nurses work on the baby. It seemed like an eternity, but finally the blue started to turn pink. He was alive!

As I peered over Marie's shoulder to look at the baby swathed in her arms, he looked into my eyes as if he was saying, "Please don't go. Stay."

Marie brought her baby, George, home to live with us. My husband was so excited to help her care for him. I, on the other hand, was reluctant. I had decided I did not want to get attached to this boy. I wanted my daughter to be responsible for him. I was afraid that my holding him or caring for him would take away from my daughter's bonding process. So I stayed away for the first few days, both physically and emotionally closed off.

Domingo took that boy in his arms and never wanted to put him down. He tried to get me to hold him and feed him, but I couldn't. One night my husband came to our room as I was sitting on our bed. He held the baby in front of me and said in a tiny, sweet voice, making the baby's hands move, "Mimi, look at me. I ate all my food. I'm a good boy, Mimi. I'm a good boy."

I tried to be strong.

"Mimi, look at me. I'm a good boy."

I broke down and cried and took George from Domingo's arms. Even as I write this, tears roll down my face. *You fool!* I thought as

I held this precious child. *What were you thinking?* In a flash, as I held that sweet child in my arms, I knew I would commit my life to helping raise him.

George was a difficult baby for many reasons. He was very sick and ended up in the hospital a few days after being born. When I went into intensive care to see him, I broke down. He was so tiny, so little, lying in what seemed to be an enormous crib. The doctors had him hooked up to scary monitors, and he had tubes traveling into his nose and mouth. I wondered if he would survive. He looked so weak.

We learned he had a hole in his heart and a bad valve that would eventually have to be repaired. This was a lot for all of us to process. What we didn't know was that this was just the beginning of George's many hardships. I was in no way prepared for what was ahead of us.

I came home from work one day and found Marie sitting on the floor. I could tell she had been crying. "It's all my fault, Mom."

"What is, Marie?" I said as I sat on the floor with her.

She took a deep breath and cried some more before she could speak. "It's my fault George is sick. If only I hadn't taken all those drugs ..."

"That might be true," I said softly, "but you chose life. And I am so proud of you for that."

She sat there, staring into her lap, not looking convinced.

"Marie, you need to look to the future and not the past. What's important is that you're doing the best you can for him right now." I leaned over and gave her a hug.

George was soon diagnosed with Noonan syndrome, which brings with it many medical issues, including slow growth, swallowing difficulties, and heart problems. He would be small and he would struggle with surgeries and many other things, but we loved our boy and didn't care what his medical issues were. He brought so much joy to our lives.

The dark years slowly began to fade as God used this boy to bring light to my life and to soften my hard-bitten heart. I enjoyed every waking day with him. I looked forward to our time together.

My daughter was a good mom, but I could tell she wanted out. The demons in her life were rising to the surface. She had been mishandled and ill-treated as a child, and she was wrestling with those hurts. The few times George had been hospitalized, she had been unable to cope. I told her that if she wanted to leave we would care for George. But there was one catch: if she left, I could never give him back. I told her it wouldn't be fair to him. He needed stability.

He was three the day she left for good. He chased her out the door, crying over and over, "Don't go, Mommy, don't go. I be a good boy." I didn't expect that, and I don't think my daughter did either. It was heart wrenching to watch.

One afternoon I heard this little voice saying, "Mommy, Mommy." It was a strange sound. I thought only George was home, and he called me Mimi like my other grandchildren did, so I knew it wasn't him. But I went upstairs, and there was George sitting on the top step, saying, "Mommy," over and over. When I picked him up, he looked up at me with his deep brown eyes and asked, "Are you my mommy?"

Attempting to share what I felt is extremely perplexing. I was increasingly becoming aware that this boy was special, and I believed wholeheartedly that he was a remarkable gift to us.

I held him tightly and said, "I will be anything you want me to be."

He fingered my hair, looking intently into my eyes. "Can I call you Mommy?"

My heart melted. "Of course, George. You can call me anything you want."

George was such a wonderful boy, but his sicknesses were hard on us emotionally and physically. Noonan syndrome brought many issues with it, and we had to deal with each one in turn. At the age of six, George had already been through four surgeries, two of which had not gone well.

You know the funny thing was, we were able to handle all of it. I learned from his big brother Joseph's death that God's grace doesn't come before or after a trial—it comes in the middle of it. And God kept us strong and focused and able to deal with every different thing that came along with George's health. And what we learned with him would help us in the future with other kids. We just didn't know it yet.

chapter 11

opening my heart

I had been so negative for so long, closed off to being a foster parent ever again. But my boy George began filling my dry, empty cup.

Even though he was often sick and needed many surgeries, he was such a joy. After the tough years in our home, our personal engines needed major tune-ups. God used this little pip-squeak of a boy to fix us and tune us up.

I told Domingo that I simply couldn't take one more stressful event—and then *bam!* one more thing happened. Things got so difficult for me at our church, I asked Domingo if we could find a new one. There was one in town, quite close to us, with a pastor by the name of Francis Chan, who I had heard speak at a graduation ceremony.

We began to attend there, and his sermons were powerful, his passion and excitement for living a radical life catching. It wasn't long before we were involved in starting a special-needs program for disabled kids and a support group for their parents.

Still, I kept my heels dug in. I wasn't going to go back to taking care of foster children. My heart had been broken too many times. I was tired. My knees were literally worn out.

Then our pastor went to Africa. When he returned, his passion for the needy and the orphans exploded. He shared about the poverty and the orphans in Africa, then challenged us as a congregation to make a difference in eternity by helping them.

As he spoke, God nudged me every time I heard the word *orphan*. I squirmed a lot. I didn't want to hear what God might be saying, because I didn't want to have to obey once I heard.

I loved teaching young college girls. I felt God had put that desire in my heart because I was completely in my element when I taught his Word. Yet deep in my heart I felt it was time to roll up my sleeves and get back to work; the vacation was over. I cried. I didn't like what I believed God was telling me. "I want you to take on a harder task," he said. "I want you to take in orphans and teach them. It will be through them I will teach you who I really am."

"I can't," I protested. "It's too hard."

"It's going to get harder. And when you say you *can't*, I'm going to keep putting burdens on you until you see it's my power that gets you through."

I finally surrendered and began to ask him to put the desire for orphans back in my heart.

The next Sunday during the sermon, there was a deep stirring in my soul. *Yes, Lord!* I leaned forward in my seat. What was God going to ask me to do? My heart began softening and opening again. I believed there was something more for Domingo and me. Sure, we were in our fifties, but does age really matter to God? We had much of a life of faith left to live. We didn't want to stop serving as so many others in our age group had. I started to pray for God to take us on a big adventure. I began to go into my room, get on my knees, and pray, "Lord, change our lives dramatically for you and your cause. I want to be like Paul and finish the race. I want to run until I drop and receive my heavenly prize. Put us to work where you need us most. Move us somewhere far away."

I knew that by this time, Domingo was tired of owning his own business, but I didn't think he would want to leave. So I also prayed, "Lord, put the desire in Domingo's heart to move." Every day I prayed these things, eager to see what God would do. And every Monday, while Domingo was at work, I prayed and fasted. But I never told Domingo about my prayers. I wanted to see God move without my "help." I can tell you I was very excited. I knew in my heart we would soon be doing God's work!

A few months later, our son Anthony called from his new home in Northern California. He wanted to let me know that there were advertisements and signs everywhere in the area announcing a desperate need for foster parents. "Mom," my son said, "this is where you and Dad belong."

My persistent son sent an ad from a Christian foster care agency that caught my interest. At the time, the county he lived in was number one in the nation for meth abuse, and the result was that kids were being sexually and physically abused and neglected. We discovered that there were over 450 kids needing placement in that small community alone! Talk about a change of heart! Now I was praying specifically, because I knew that was where we needed to go.

a big move

About a year after I started praying and fasting, Domingo came home and told me there had to be more to life than what he'd been doing. I hadn't shared my prayers with him, so it was almost unbelievable when he said that maybe we should think about moving. It was thrilling seeing God work in his heart too! Being in our fifties and owning a business, we knew it wouldn't be an easy transition. But we also knew that if God wanted this, no one could stop it.

We decided to follow up on our son's invitation and took a trip to Northern California to explore the area and meet with the Christian foster care agency. As we drove up the mountain, we had a sense of excitement mixed with fear. Our meeting with the Christian foster care agency went well, as did our time looking at properties. We discovered a house on three wooded acres outside town that had much potential for a large family. By the end of our stay, we knew this was where we needed to be.

Domingo and I drove home, giddy with excitement and spilling over with ideas of what we would do. We weren't sure we could afford the house. The price difference from what we thought we would receive in equity from our house sale in Simi Valley and what this house would cost was significant. We certainly didn't have jobs lined up in the area, and we knew the house would need a lot of work to make it more suitable for taking in kids, so we had to be extrawise with our finances. However, we knew that if God wanted us to move north and have this home, he would work it out.

Many of the people at home quickly dampened our excitement. When we shared our new venture with them, some thought we were nuts and discouraged us from following our convictions. Thankfully, our close friends embraced and encouraged us. Even so, we wanted to be sure we weren't being foolish, so we went to talk to our pastor and asked him if he thought we were being sober minded in our thinking. Francis's encouraging and enthusiastic response of "Yeah! Go for it!" really sealed the deal for us.

As the excitement wore off and the tasks of moving so far away cluttered my to-do list, I started to get cold feet about using all our money for this venture. It would mean not putting away any money for retirement. People's comments about the foolishness of our choice added to my concerns. A sweet friend waved off all the negative comments by saying, "Irene, you are investing in eternity. Your return will be from God, and it will be huge." Perfect words at the perfect time. God would take care of us as he always had.

Before we could go anywhere, we had to sell our house and our business. We spoke to a broker, and he told us it would take at least a year to a year and a half to sell the business. The residential real estate market in Simi was good.

The first day our house was officially on the market, we held an open house. Seven groups of people came through, each one putting in an offer, and each offer higher than the last. All the offers were much higher than we expected. The difference between what we thought we'd get for the house and what we did get was, of course, the exact amount we needed to get the house up north. Then our business sold right away as well.

With packed boxes piled high around us in our Simi Valley kitchen, we began to fill out our application for foster parenting. George was very excited because he was tired of being the only child in the family and had been praying for new brothers and sisters for quite some time.

We sent our application ahead of us, finished our packing, and made the big move. It had been only six weeks from the time we made the decision to move. Only God could have orchestrated that. It was hard for even us to believe, and we were right there, watching it all happen. Now, more than ever, we knew God had a plan for us up north. And we felt privileged that he was going to use us.

The first week in our new home, we met with the social worker. I reminded her we wanted only short-term kids who we could help in the reunification process with their parents. I made sure I emphasized the fact that I didn't want long-term kids. I didn't tell her that was because taking in long-term kids was too risky. I didn't want to fall in love with them. And I *really* didn't want to adopt.

In anticipation of the kids to come, we bought bunk beds for two rooms and moved Esther to the loft that later became our schoolroom. Because Domingo now didn't have a job, I planned to keep mine in Southern California for at least a year. Sure, it was a long commute, but I'd drive down on Wednesdays and drive back on Sundays.

The day I drove down for my first commute, the social worker brought a sibling group of four—one boy age nine and three girls ages seven, five, and three—to Domingo. Thankfully, Esther, now twenty-two, had moved with us and could help Domingo with the kids.

How did Domingo do? Probably better than I would have. He's always been marvelous with kids. Even more proof of God's good work in this man's heart.

Domingo was never one to sit still. The house needed so much work, and he didn't waste a moment getting started. Every time I came home from Southern California, he had done something new. I'd come home to find a tractor. Then the next time I came home, the tractor was gone, and a section of the property had been cleared. The next time, there was a playground. And when I was home, he worked in his new handyman business.

When the first sibling group left after about five months, saying good-bye was extremely agonizing. As we watched the car pull out of our driveway, we were all sad—almost brokenhearted. So much for not getting attached. This was lesson 101 in foster parenting. We were definitely learning—and not liking it very much.

After the kids left, George started praying for brothers and sisters. And a few kids did come, but not as many as we'd expected when we started this journey. They'd come one at a time and be at our home for a week or two.

Although I'd planned to commute to Southern California for a year, the distance and amount of work to be done at home began to take their toll on me. The owner of the salon was very gracious to release me from my obligations in September. I was so grateful. However, I didn't have a job near my home and knew I would need to find one as soon as I could. It didn't take long before I found a small salon where I could begin my work part-time.

That fall, siblings Bobby and Missy arrived. They were a handful at first. Missy was three, soon to be four, and boy, did she have the gift of gab. Bobby was about seven, was tough, and kept an eye on his little sister, sweetly taking care of her. They had separate visits with each of their parents. Mom was usually high and despised us, and Dad was kind, thanking us for caring for his children.

We were settling in to our new home. Domingo and I were a lot stronger and were ready for our new venture, praying for the children God was going to bring us. We knew Bobby and Missy would be leaving soon; their reunification process with their dad was going well. They would be leaving to go live with him in a few months.

Then one cool September night, the phone rang.

PART 3

RICH IN LOVE

♡

chapter 12

a new journey begins

2004

When I answered the phone, I recognized the social worker's voice immediately. "I have a four-year-old little boy who has never been in the system. He was picked up from a meth raid, and he's pretty frightened."

I looked over at Domingo, and he nodded. "Of course," I said to the worker. Not long after the call, we opened the door to the social worker, who was escorting a little boy with pure white hair down to his shoulders, rotten teeth, and a filthy mess of dirt caked on him. He had on some sort of water shoes, and he stank. I don't know what I had expected, but I was shocked. The excitement of bringing in this child left, and fear took over. For a moment I didn't know what to do, but then autopilot kicked in. "Come on, let's go take a bath."

He just looked at me, eyes wide. He didn't say a word. Turns out he couldn't talk well. Not only did he not have a very big vocabulary, he didn't seem to know how to go up the stairs. He fumbled and looked confused and frightened at the same time.

I helped him get up the stairs to the big bathtub in our bedroom. I turned on the water, stripped off his clothes, and got him into the tub. He started to shriek and wail in a high-pitched sound so penetrating, our neighbors (whose homes are a distance from ours) could hear him. They said it made their blood curdle.

"Shhhh," I said quietly, soothingly. "It's okay. You're safe here." I slowly ran the water over his body with a washcloth, going deaf from his shrieks.

I thought I saw something crawling on his head and called, "Mingo! We need lice treatment." Domingo went to the garage to the stash we had on hand and brought me a box. I had put on gloves and wrapped a hair-cutting drape around me to protect my clothes from the water and pesticide. Once the little boy's hair got wet and flat, I could see a city of lice in his hair. I have seen a lot of scalp problems in my years as a hairstylist, but this was by far the most disgusting, disturbing thing I have ever seen.

I was dying inside and started to feel bugs crawling up my arms—whether they were or not. Throughout all the screaming, I kept bathing and rinsing, bathing and rinsing, five or six times, as well as giving him the lice treatment.

Then I saw something weird on the side of the tub. Looking closer, I screamed, "*Domingo!*" and added my shriek to the poor little boy's as I watched lice crawling up the sides of the tub.

Domingo came quickly, looked at where I was pointing, and, as I wrapped the boy in a towel and helped him out, cleaned it up.

I wanted to pick the boy up and hug him to comfort him, but he was so infested that I held back. Instead, I took him to the garage and shaved off all his hair—which made him start the screeching sound again. This poor little guy had scabs all over his head from the biting bugs. It was really gross. He was only four, and he had to endure all this—and so much more we had no idea about.

I put the few pieces of clothing he arrived with into a trash bag, tied it up, and tossed it. One of the many rules for caring for foster kids is that you aren't supposed to throw the kids' clothes away. I didn't care. I couldn't have those lice infecting our entire household—or risk getting meth into our systems through contact with the contaminated clothing.

After we got clean clothes on this terrified little guy, George, now eight, put his arm around him and said, "Don't be afraid, buddy. Do you want some milk and Oreos?"

"Gulk," the little boy said over and over. "Gulk."

Together the boys ate cookies, but it was clear the new little boy had never had an Oreo before. He was mesmerized, watching George carefully as he twisted the cookie, pulled it apart, and licked the frosting from the inside. The boy picked up one and did exactly as George had, never taking his eyes off him. I wasn't sure how he ate the cookies at all. His teeth were rotten nearly to the gums.

"It's gonna be okay, buddy," George said over and over, calming the boy down. "Nothing's going to happen. We've been praying for you."

We learned his name was Kurt, and he had created his own language beyond his limited English vocabulary that we couldn't remotely understand.

Before putting him to bed in George's room, I encouraged him to use the toilet. As I closed the door between us I said, "Don't forget to wipe."

He was in the bathroom for a long time, and I got concerned. I tapped on the door a couple of times. "Kurt? Kurt, honey, are you okay?"

No answer.

After the third time, I opened the door and saw poop all over his hand and arm. Sometimes something catches you so off guard that you say something you wouldn't have if you'd been prepared. "Kurt, are you kidding me?" I said. "What were you thinking? Didn't you use the toilet paper?"

He looked at me, confused, eyes wide. I pointed to the paper, and he answered in a voice that sounded like a deaf boy's. "I don't know how." Then it dawned on me. He didn't know what toilet paper was for!

We gave him another bath. By the time we were done, it was really late. When I tucked him into bed, he said in that same odd voice, "I miss my mama."

As always happened when a child came to us, my heart broke for this little lost child torn from his family and plunked down in a stranger's house. I went to bed, not knowing what to do for him, and fell asleep with prayers for wisdom on my lips.

Within a day or so the foster agency let us know what Kurt's visitation schedule would be. We took him to the small building in town where parents could have supervised visits with their children, and he seemed apprehensive. When his parents came into the room, they awkwardly reached out to hug him, but he clearly didn't want them to touch him. He backed away, fear in his eyes. That seemed so strange to me. Most children, no matter how crazy their situation, still want their parents. Even stranger, within a week, he wasn't asking for his mama and didn't want to see her.

As the weeks passed, it became clear he'd had little training in the basics of life. The foster agency called him a feral child. Alone and neglected, he had mostly raised himself. As a result, he hated to be touched and would go into rages.

One night he woke, screaming. I ran to him and held him. "I was on the TV," he cried. The next words came out slowly, and he stumbled over a lot of them. "The man had a camera. He took pictures of me. I was on the TV. The man was hurting me." In time he would tell us more and that his father had been involved. The events, explained from a child's perspective, were graphic even in their simplicity. You can imagine what those things were and how they would impact a small child.

His mom said she wanted him back, but she showed up to the visits high as a kite. She didn't do anything the court had ordered her to do so she could regain custody of her son. Meth is such a wicked drug. This woman had come from a good, wealthy family and had a master's degree—yet the drug had consumed her until she lived only for getting high. Nothing else mattered. Not even her son.

At visitations, Kurt continued to flinch or stiffen when his parents tried to touch him. It seemed clear his parents hadn't hugged him much, if at all. They were awkward in how they approached him, and he appeared to be unfamiliar and uncomfortable with what they were doing. Soon, when I'd take him to see his parents, he wouldn't want to get out of the car. During the visits he'd rage, screaming his high-pitched scream that put fear into grown men.

During those first six months, I fell in love with this unusual little boy. Despite the abuse he'd experienced, he had such an innocence about him, untainted by the world. And, oh, how he loved George. That relationship was clearly comforting for him. But I hurt for him because of the unimaginable pain he'd gone through.

One night after he'd had a nightmare, I said, "Kurt, do you want to pray?"

"What's that?" he said in his thick voice.

"It's when we talk to God."

"Who's that?"

"Don't you know who God is? Who Jesus is?"

"No."

I couldn't believe that this boy had no understanding of anything spiritual. How could he not know who God is? I explained in as simple terms as possible that God was his Father and he created everything in the world. I told him about God's Son, Jesus, and all the things he did for us. Kurt couldn't talk very well, but I knew he understood. I explained what prayer is, and then I prayed with him.

He believed the gospel immediately and completely. There was no hesitation, no question that this was right. He accepted that God was with us even though he couldn't see him. From that moment, Kurt's faith began to grow. And I could see what Jesus meant when he talked about childlike faith in Matthew 18:4: "Anyone who becomes as humble as this little child is the greatest in the Kingdom of Heaven."

There are many people who study God's Word for years but still don't understand this message. This simple, feral child did! There was nothing to cloud or confuse this boy's faith. He took the things we taught him about God and his Word as truth. If I said God loved him and took care of him, then he believed God loved him and took care of him.

Kurt's faith put me to shame. Why couldn't I learn to trust God in that simple, childlike way? I complicate my Christianity with too much stuff—and Christ's message is really uncomplicated. I have to remind myself he didn't use the educated Pharisees and scribes to share his message—he chose unqualified, uneducated fishermen. I forget I have all I need when I study God's Word and see him in action.

chapter 13

blessed be your name

A few months after Kurt arrived, George developed a sore throat, so I took him to the immediate care clinic. The doctor told me he wanted to X-ray George's lungs. I thought that was strange. Why would he want to X-ray his lungs when he had a sore throat? *He probably just wants our money.*

The doctor didn't tell me that he'd heard something unusual while listening to George's breathing and wanted to check it out. After taking George's X-ray, he gave us antibiotics and sent us home.

About a week later, the clinic doctor called, asking us to come in and get another X-ray. "I found a large spot on George's X-ray, and I want to make sure it's a spot on the film and not a tumor."

What? My world stopped, and I was frozen in time, unable to think, feel, or hear. Immediately, I took George to get his X-ray retaken.

"Mrs. Garcia," the doctor said after he'd called me into his office, his face somber, "you need to take your son to a pediatric oncologist right away. There's a good chance George has cancer."

My whole body shuddered. An alarming sense of fear encompassed every ounce of my being. The words *my boy has cancer* relentlessly ran over and over through my mind. I was terrified. Shaking, I called Domingo. I could barely get the words out—"They think George has cancer"—before I started to cry. Tenderhearted Domingo also started to cry for our boy.

I met the oncologist in Sacramento, a nearly two-hour drive from our home. He gave me the grim news. "It looks like your son has a malignant tumor in his lungs."

In a matter of hours they put George through all kinds of tests, and the diagnosis went from bad to worse. The oncologist did not give us much hope. I left the office to call everyone I knew at Cornerstone Church. They in turn called others, and the twenty-four-hour prayer covering for George began.

I needed to get home to care for Bobby, Missy, and Kurt, so Domingo started on the long drive down to be with George. That began a new tag-team system we had to use throughout George's illness.

Both home and hospital were tough for me to deal with physically and emotionally. Kurt was a mess. He didn't understand what was going on. The big brother he loved—who was his entire world—was suddenly no longer around, and Kurt was lost without him. Kurt was still so new to us, still struggling to understand the simplest things in life, as well as with going to the hated visitations with his parents. Bobby and Missy were going to their separate visitations, and then we had to deal with the emotional fallout from those visits. And being with George was a whole different type of physical and emotional trial.

One morning on my long drive to the hospital, I cried and pleaded with God. My mother had died of lung cancer within a few months of her diagnosis, so I believed George did not have long to live. "Why does my boy have to go through all of this? Why are you taking him, God?" I also said some not-nice things, letting it all out, holding nothing back. After all, God says to bring all our petitions to him, even our hurts and anger, so I was just being obedient!

"You already took one son. Why are you going to take this one too?"

Then the song "Blessed Be Your Name" by Matt Redman came through the speakers. As I heard the lyrics repeated—"You give and take away, you give and take away; my heart will choose to say, Lord, blessed be your name"—I realized I had been focusing on my circumstances and not on my blessings. George was God's child; I was the steward assigned to care for him. God let me have George for eight years, and if he chose to take him, I would be forever thankful for the time George had been in our care.

The more I listened to the song and prayed, my pain slowly turned into joy because I trusted my God.

When I got to the hospital, the doctor told me he had good news. After running all the tests, they could see that George's tumor was on his ribs behind his lungs, rather than inside the lungs. God answered my prayers. I had hope. George had a chance.

The grapefruit-sized tumor would take eight hours of surgery. Afterward, George would go through chemotherapy. I marveled that a week before, I was panicked because there was a spot on an X-ray, and now I was praising God that my son could go through chemotherapy.

As we sat on George's hospital bed after they'd done the initial prep for his surgery, George looked at me with his warm brown eyes and said, "Mom, am I going to die?"

I have always been honest with my kids, so I had to tell him the truth. "Yes, George, there's a possibility you will die." I pulled him close. "Are you ready to stand before God?"

"I'm not sure."

"Do you want to be sure?" I pulled away from him and looked at him closely. "If so, we can pray."

He nodded. We bowed our heads. We prayed, and George made Jesus the Lord of his life.

Domingo and I sat in the waiting room while George was in surgery. "Domingo, do you think George is going to die?"

"No, Irene. I feel George will be okay." He smiled. Once again this man's confidence was a blessing to me. "Just keep praying." He grabbed my hand, giving me the confidence I needed not to fear but to hope.

I prayed most of the time George was in surgery, and while I was praying I felt the Spirit saying to me, "George will be healed." I thought my emotions were playing tricks on me, but I chose to believe anyway.

When the doctor finally came out, we were anxious to hear the news. It was, like most news of its type, both good and bad. "George's ribs are so full of holes they look like Pac-Man has been in there eating them up," he told us. "We couldn't get it all, but the chemotherapy will take care of the rest of the cancer." He paused a moment as he looked at each of us. "I took a biopsy. I'm sure it was malignant because of how aggressive it was. We should have the results of the biopsy in a few days."

"Will he be okay?"

"With treatment, yes, he should be fine."

All I could think was, *Our boy is alive!*

I couldn't wait to go sit with George as he recuperated from surgery. "Son," I said the day after his surgery, "it's evident God has a plan for your life. After all, this isn't the first time God has been by your side, saving your life."

He looked at me, his eyes wide, and he slowly nodded as he took in everything I said.

I took both his hands in mine. "You need to find your purpose in life and seek God's will."

"How, Mom?"

"Talk to God. Ask him to show you."

George stayed in the hospital for ten days. Each time someone came in to check on him, we asked about the results of the biopsy. "The results will be in any day now" was the answer we kept getting. Well, "any day" turned into another week, then two, then three. When I called the lab, they told me they had to keep sending it back to be reevaluated because something was wrong. I knew people must still be praying for us because I wasn't anxious.

It was about a month before the surgeon's office called and wanted to see us about the biopsy results. That's rarely a good sign. They usually give bad news in person. George and I drove the long distance, not talking much. Yet, again, I didn't feel the anxiety I had when George was first diagnosed. I sang the words to "Blessed Be Your Name" in my head.

When the surgeon came into his office, he had a funny look on his face. He sat behind his desk and opened a thick file folder and flipped through the first few pages. I tried to be patient, trying to figure out what that expression on his face meant.

"Well," the surgeon said, closing the folder, "the biopsy came back negative. There are no signs of cancer."

I flushed with joy. "That's wonderful! But why aren't you happy? Is there something else wrong?"

"Mrs. Garcia, I do surgeries like this all the time. I saw the tumor. This one was especially aggressive. I *know* it was cancerous." He shook his head, folding his hands on his desk. "I have no explanation for it."

I leaned toward him across the desk. "I know what happened. God healed my son. When he was in surgery, I felt God's Spirit tell me George would be healed. I know it's hard for you to understand, but my God is the great physician."

His eyes watered up, and then tears ran down his cheeks, but he said nothing.

"I'm a Christian, and there's nothing you can say that will change this truth."

I went home and continued to pray for the doctor, hoping we made an impact in his life.

About six years later, a woman came to town for a conference. She saw our salon and stepped in to see if she could get a haircut. I had a cancellation, so she was given to me. As I worked and we chatted, we discovered she was related to George's surgeon. The woman was a Christian. She told me the surgeon had walked away from God. Then about six years ago, a patient had made an impact on his life, and now he was following God.

I told her our story. She said we must be the people he'd talked about because the stories were similar. She fully believed God used us in this man's life.

You see why I keep taking in kids? God uses them to show me he is alive and working in our midst. How can I keep this a secret? I want to shout it to the ends of the earth! If I don't leave my comfort zone and step out in faith, I will never experience the miracles God keeps showing me when I trust.

Through this trial with George, I also saw how my joy did not have to come from circumstances; it is a supernatural gift from God that comes when I begin to trust and praise him. Philippians 4:4 says, "Rejoice in the Lord always; again I will say, rejoice!" (NASB). First Peter 1:6 says, "In this you greatly rejoice, even though now for a little while, if necessary, you have been distressed by various trials" (NASB).

God does not tell us to do something we are unable to do without his help! My hope is that when I go through trials people will see the joy in me. I know I will continue to cry, and the heartaches will come, but in the end I will have joy in my God and the salvation he has given me.

Kurt's issues

George continued to recover, though he still required frequent visits to the oncologist in Sacramento. Bobby and Missy went to live with their father and grandmother. It took some time, but the scabs on Kurt's head went away and we got his rotten teeth fixed. An emotional healing process was occurring in him as well, and we could see him learning to trust his new family. However, there were some odd things about him. One was that he didn't want to be touched by anyone but me. And then there were his cars. The only thing that kid could talk about was cars. At four, he knew every model and car symbol. But it went beyond that.

"I'm pretty sure he's autistic," I told the agency. "He puts his cars in order, then moves them out, then puts them back in order, then moves them out. Over and over."

They told me this was common with kids who have been abused. "He wants to be in control," they said.

"No," I said. "Out of all the kids, he's the only one who *doesn't* want to be in control. Yes, he wants to be in *charge*, but not *control*. There's a difference." Kurt loved being given a job to be in charge of. He was precise and meticulous about completing the job he'd been given, but he didn't need to be in *control* of things in general.

"Look," I insisted, "there's something wrong with him."

No one believed me. Although I hadn't been around him for more than six months, I still knew this boy. I refused to settle for what they told me. Because I had been involved in special-needs ministry for many years, I had cared for many autistic children. Kurt had so many similar tendencies. I wanted him to be diagnosed so he could get the help he needed. Although we went to a special clinic, the doctors stuck with the mentally delayed diagnosis because he was unable to communicate very well and his movements were awkward and extremely clumsy.

At that point I let it go. My job was to keep loving and training this boy. Domingo and I would find his strengths and build him up from there. We would trust God to show us what to do next.

Kurt was growing by leaps and bounds. Sometimes he would even let me hug him. One day without thinking, I grabbed him and said, "Give me a kiss, handsome! Lay one on me, right there." I turned my head and tapped my cheek. "Come on," I said, laughing. "Smack it on right here."

Instead of giggling and giving me a peck like most kids did, he looked at me and then put his head down. There was a look of panic on his face.

"What's the matter, Kurt?"

His blue eyes wide, he shrugged his shoulders and gave me his mumbled answer for everything. "I don't know."

"Come on, Kurt, smack it on your mama right here." I could tell he felt unsure but not uncomfortable. "Don't you want to give me a kiss?"

He tried to pucker his lips, but he couldn't do it. And then it hit me—he didn't know *how* to kiss.

So I said, "Kurt, do you know how to kiss? Have you ever kissed anybody?"

"No ..." He dragged the word out.

"Come here, Son." I grabbed him and kissed him all over his head and face and said, "*That's* how you kiss!"

I told him to try to kiss my cheek. His struggle was heart wrenching to watch. He had to put a lot of thought into what he was trying to do. He had to work hard, but he finally gave me a kiss. I had never known a child who couldn't kiss. How many people have to teach their children to kiss them?

chapter 14

Raymond and Samantha

wisdom

By March 2005, although George was cancer-free, we still needed to take him back and forth to the oncologist. Kurt was progressing, although still having difficult visits with his parents. One afternoon, the social services agency called. "We have two kids—a boy and a girl—who have been in a temporary shelter for a month. Both parents are in jail, and we can't find a placement. Would you consider taking them?"

Even though Domingo wasn't home, I knew what his answer would be. "Yes, of course we will."

They told me the boy, Raymond, was sixteen months and the girl, Samantha, was about to turn three. Would I be able to pick them up?

I was able to reach Domingo, and he was just as excited as I was. We wanted to fill our home to the brim with children.

As I drove our van to the county pickup office, I was excited. I guess I always got excited knowing God was answering our prayers to make a difference in the lives of kids. So when the opportunities came, we were ready and eager.

I parked the van and went inside, especially excited to meet the little girl. The social worker approached me, holding this little girl with a pixie haircut and bright green eyes that grabbed me. As I reached out to receive this precious gift, my heart leaped with joy and my eyes filled with tears. I couldn't believe it. She was such an itty-bitty thing who so easily came into my arms, an innocent child trusting and embracing me, someone she didn't know. Conflicting emotions flooded through me: anger, fear, love, joy, and hatred of those who would harm her. At that moment I knew my purpose in life: to help the defenseless.

Then another social worker came through a door, holding the boy. The moment I saw him I thought, *He is the ugliest baby I have ever seen.* He looked at me almost like he was dazed, his tongue hanging out of his mouth like a thirsty little puppy dog. He didn't cry, but his eyes were watering as I buckled him into the child's seat in the back. The girl also didn't cry when we put her in her seat. She just looked at me with those beautiful green eyes. She was so tiny—almost frail looking—but she had the most beautiful smile.

As I drove home, I kept looking at Raymond through the rearview mirror, baffled at his hanging tongue. I'd never seen a baby do that before, and nobody had told me why it was protruding like that. I thought about how most babies have a sweet look, but this one just looked mean and *mad*. He didn't seem to be the least bit afraid. But there was something in his eyes that caused a stirring in my stomach. He looked so stinking tough. I started praying for these little children, asking God for wisdom. I knew they had been through a lot;

I just didn't know yet what that was. At the very least it had been a month since they had seen their mom.

When we got home, the first thing I did was give them each a quick bath. The little guy didn't cry. He stiffened his whole body as though he was saying, *Go ahead and try.* On the other hand, the little girl was all smiles and hugs, as though she had known me her whole life. When it was time to put on Raymond's diaper, I grabbed his ankles to lift him. And then I saw them. Boils. Lots of open, festering boils. His bottom was raw, almost like one open wound. I got really upset and called the county immediately. "Why does this boy have these boils?" I demanded.

"The boils are actually getting better," the worker told me. I thought, *No way are they getting better. Somebody wasn't on top of this.*

When Domingo came home, I was sitting outside on the grass and Esther was sitting on the steps, holding Samantha.

"Is this our new little guy?" he asked, taking Samantha from Esther's arms.

"No, Mingo. This is our girl, Samantha."

"Hello, Samantha," he said. "I'm Papi." She grinned at him— again, as if she'd known him her whole life.

"Mingo, you've got to see this," I said. I took him into the bedroom, where Raymond was waking up from his nap. I put Raymond on our bed to change his diaper and showed Domingo.

He was so upset. "Who would allow this to happen to a baby?"

We took him to a doctor right away and found out he had a staph infection. We got the prescribed ointment. It took nearly a year for his poor little bottom to heal. We believe that was one of the reasons why he didn't want to be held or touched—it hurt.

A few days after Raymond and Samantha came to stay with us, we were informed that their mom had gotten out of jail and was scheduled to have a visit with them. The moment we arrived for visitation, it was clear Samantha *loved* her mom. She took off running to her at full speed, screaming and yelling with excitement, and threw herself into her mother's arms for hugs and kisses and all sorts of sweetness between the two of them. The children's grandmother stood to one side and took emotionless Raymond from me. Mom didn't pay the least bit of attention to Raymond, aside from giving him some candy and a liter of soda that she had brought for both of them.

This became the pattern for every visit. When the visits ended, both kids were wound up from a sugar high. I was not a happy camper, but Samantha loved those visits and the attention she received from her mom. She was so clingy and wanted all the attention for herself. That didn't seem to bother Raymond in the least. He didn't want anything to do with his mother.

When the visits ended, Samantha became completely distraught, screaming, and crying, "Don't go! I don't want my mommy to go!"

It was horrible. Can you imagine what was going on in her little mind? I was tearing her from her mommy, saying gently but firmly, "Come on, Samantha. It's time to go." I'm sure that little girl saw me as the enemy since I continually took her away from her mother. I didn't even know how to console her. My heart was pleading, *Please, God, no more visits.* But my mind was reminding me, *This is her mother!*

At home, Samantha frequently asked about her mom, her grandma, and her grandmother's horse. She demanded a lot of attention, wanting to be loved and hugged constantly and wanting me all to herself. Although she had a sweet, teachable spirit, she was also disobedient, sometimes throwing tantrums, screaming and crying. That didn't bother me much. I knew it was normal—especially with foster kids.

On the other hand, Raymond didn't want anything from us. After his first week he started to show some personality. Only it wasn't warm and fuzzy. He just wanted all of us to get out of his way so he could be left alone to do his own thing. And when he got mad, he threw horrible fits and tantrums where he'd fling himself backward. You could hear the crack as the back of his head smacked the hard tile. He kicked and screamed and bit. His little body was so thick and muscular, it looked like he was strutting about when he walked. If you have ever seen the Foghorn Leghorn cartoon, he was like the tough little Chicken Hawk who bossed around the big rooster. The only difference was Raymond didn't talk. In fact, he didn't talk for another year. And if I wrote his first words, this book would have to be X-rated. Since they were words we never speak, I knew he had picked them up from his past.

When he was upset, it was impossible to console him. I wanted to love on him, but he wouldn't allow it. Eventually I was at my wit's end. I fell to my knees in the closet. "God, I need wisdom for this boy. I don't know what to do. How can I help him?"

I walked into the kitchen with the sense of prayer surrounding me. A bag of chocolate caramels sat on the kitchen counter. And it came to me. These two kids obviously *loved* sugar, since their diet with their mom seemed to be full of it. So I tucked a caramel in my pocket, found Raymond, and took him to the rocking chair. He screamed bloody murder and stiffened. He fought me and fought me. I calmly unwrapped the caramel and stuck it in his mouth. Within moments, I could feel his little body start to soften, then he totally surrendered and relaxed in my arms. I was so jazzed that I rocked him until he fell asleep.

Oh, how I was praising God! *God, I'm so silly. Here I was knocking myself out, trying to figure out what to do with this baby boy, and all I needed to do was to ask you. You gave me the wisdom, God! It was you!*

I felt like I heard God say, "Irene, all you needed to do was ask."

Boy, was that ever a lesson for me. It's not complicated like I try to make it. It's simple. Every time I'm stumped, I need to get on my knees. These are God's children, and he knows what to do.

I continued to work with Raymond. I'd get the candy and say, "Come on, Raymond." I'd take him to the chair, and he'd fight me and fight me while I tried to hold him. Then I'd give him the caramel, and he'd start to relax. After a while, when we got into the rocker, he'd start relaxing automatically, waiting for the candy. Pretty soon I didn't even need the candy. I could pick him up, hold him, and rock him. I felt like we were finally connecting. And from that point on, he started to blossom.

Memorial Day weekend, 2005

For about two and a half months we'd been taking Raymond and Samantha three times a week to visit their mom and taking Kurt twice a week to visit his parents. Raymond and Samantha's mom had become erratic in her visits. We didn't know if she'd even show up, but when she did, she'd likely be high and well equipped with candies, cookies, and liters of soda pop. Her mother came with her; you could tell the grandmother loved her granddaughter very much. But neither Grandma nor Mom ever went for Raymond; they only went for Samantha, paying no attention to Raymond. Raymond acted as though he didn't even know his mom.

I went to God on my knees and pleaded with him to stop the visits, but they continued. I called the social worker and told her that I suspected the mom was high on meth during the visits. Could they please have her tested?

I don't know why the social worker didn't do anything about it for so long. She was new, so I don't know if she didn't believe me or was too busy—social workers' caseloads are so big. It took weeks before she came to observe visitation. When she saw the situation, I was sure she was going to tell me that the visits would change. Instead, she told me she had authorized the kids to go on an unsupervised three-day weekend over Memorial Day with the mom and her new boyfriend—who had a current police record. It took every ounce of self-control not to throw my own tantrum.

The social worker finally relented and ordered the mom to have a drug test on the Tuesday before the planned visit. My social worker called on Thursday to tell me I was right. Mom had tested positive. I was relieved, figuring they'd cancel the visit. But since the other social worker was on vacation and she had authorized the visit, there was no canceling it. I was dying inside, praying and pleading with God. *Lord, something bad is going to happen to these kids during this visit. I know it. Please protect them.*

When the mom picked up the kids on Friday, I was sick inside. I had to hand over two little babies to a mom high on meth and her boyfriend. All I could do was pray for their protection. And I did. I was uncomfortable the entire three days, feeling like something was going to happen. I cried and pleaded with God to let me keep these babies and protect them.

When I went to pick up the kids on Sunday, my heart was anxious, eager to see those babies. I was taken aback by my strong emotions—I had fallen madly in love with them!

As I pulled into the county agency parking lot, I knew right away something was wrong. Grandma was with the kids, not Mom. The court had ordered the mom to be with the kids at all times. Rage began to build inside of me. I marched up to the grandmother's car with quite the attitude. I opened the door to let the kids out and said, "Where's their mother? She's supposed to give me the kids, not you." I think it was a matter of seconds before I had the kids out of her car and into mine. I was furious.

I got in the car and started to drive away. Before I could get out of the parking lot, conviction swept over me. I had been rude and mean. "What did I just do?" I groaned softly. "Oh, Lord, please forgive me."

Completely ashamed, I turned the car around and parked close to the grandmother's. Her head was down, forehead against the steering wheel. She was obviously crying.

"Give me wisdom and the words to say to this woman, Lord."

I tapped lightly on her window. She unrolled it, then looked at her hands gripping the wheel, not at me. "What's wrong?" I asked.

"My daughter is going to lose these kids, and I love them so much. I don't want her to lose them. I don't want to lose my grandkids."

What could I say? I couldn't tell her that things would be okay. "You know," I said, my hatred and anger beginning to fade, "I can't tell you what's going to happen, but what I can tell you is that as long as the kids stay with us, they will be loved."

She took a deep breath and looked at me with big, sad eyes and said softly, "I know."

"I'm sorry for the way I acted. That wasn't right or fair."

She looked away and nodded.

I said, "I don't know if you know that you can turn to Jesus and give him your burdens." She didn't respond, so I turned and walked away, thinking that not only did I no longer feel hatred for this woman, but I felt compassion for her. And I couldn't help thinking how, blindsided by my anger, I had judged this poor woman. She was probably the only one really watching out for these kids. Instead of being rude to her, I should have said, "Thank you."

I never saw her again.

Samantha's revelation

When we got home, I could tell something was up with Samantha. She wasn't acting herself—she was too quiet. After visits with their parents, kids have a really hard time readjusting to the routine in our home, so I wasn't completely surprised by her behavior. Yet something was still a bit unsettling. When we went for the first supervised visit a few days later, little Samantha, who had adored her mom, was very distant from her.

A few days after that, Samantha, who had turned three in April, began to talk again. Only now she was talking about sexual things.

She had never talked like this before her weekend visitation, so I called the social worker and told her the things Samantha was saying. That call led to an investigation. To say I was angry with the sickening results of that investigation is putting it mildly. I started fighting to stop the visits.

Samantha's inappropriate behavior and talk increased. I knew she was acting out as a result of her abuse, but I simply couldn't have her openly acting out in this way in front of the other children.

Whenever foster children begin acting out, the social workers and psychologists will offer advice. As you can imagine, there is a lot of free thinking involved in the suggestions, and everyone seems to have a different opinion or solution. Most encouraged me to allow Samantha to share what she had seen and been involved in whenever and however she wanted. When we did this, though, she talked about these things *all the time.* It was clear I couldn't listen to some of the advice I'd received. It simply wasn't wise. I had to get Samantha to stop her inappropriate talk and behavior. And frankly, there were times when I was less than patient with her.

I went to my favorite place for wisdom. "Please, Lord," I begged, "give me wisdom to handle this situation with Samantha. I don't know what to do. You allowed it, and I'm stumped! You've got to help me."

First, God gave me a different wisdom. He gently pointed out that Samantha was only behaving as she had been recently taught. She didn't know any better. God was teaching me to be patient and to look at things from a different perspective by taking the blinders off my eyes. I felt so foolish for not looking outside my little box. I continued to pray for wisdom, and I was confident now that God would show me the right way to handle the situation.

Samantha was loving all the attention she was getting when she said or did these things, so no matter how much we tried to steer her in a different direction, she talked to anyone who would listen. Later that week, she began having one of these conversations with a friend of ours.

"Samantha," I said, interrupting her, "I want you to go to your room."

She went up the stairs, and I followed. I sat with her on her bed and began the conversation we'd had many times before. "Samantha, it's okay to share those things with Papi and me. We will always listen. But it's not appropriate for you to talk about those things with others."

She sat, wide-eyed, listening, but she was so little. How could she really understand? And I didn't want to tell her sex is bad; I just needed to teach her God's view of it. So I said, "God wants only married people to talk about sexual things. And since Papi and I have asked you many times to stop talking about inappropriate things, perhaps it's time for me to find you a husband so you can get married. We'll miss you very much, but this way you will be able to talk about anything you want with him. I will go call the social worker to find you one. We are going to miss you so much."

She cried, "Please, Mimi, I don't want to get married. I promise I won't talk about it to anyone except you."

It worked. She stopped sharing things openly and came to me whenever she was struggling. Praise God once again for his wisdom!

the girls and the stories

June 2005

I didn't have a lot of time to focus on Samantha's new issue because it wasn't more than a week later that we got a call about three girls who were being detained with their mom at the jail. You'd think that with Samantha's struggles we wouldn't want to take on more children. But without hesitation we said, "Of course."

Within the hour the social worker pulled into our driveway. Two little girls got out of the car while the social worker unbuckled the third from a car seat.

All three girls were filthy. They wore no shoes, and their feet were black. The middle one's hair smelled horrible and looked like it had never been combed. The baby was out of it, her eyes glazed over. The eldest walked by, seething. If she could have killed me with her eyes, she would have. The middle one was completely freaking out, flailing all over the place.

Kurt was in his room playing with his cars—he got nervous about kids coming—while George, Raymond, and Samantha watched from the staircase.

I took the limp and lethargic baby from the social worker, who told me that the baby's name was Rose and she was sixteen months old. "The older one is Elaine. She's five, almost six, and the middle one is Evelyn. She's also five—her birthday was last month."

"Hello, girls," I said, trying to be soothing and safe for them. I walked the girls past George and wide-eyed Raymond and Samantha to get them into the tub while the social worker sat with Domingo in the kitchen.

I felt this unexplainable helplessness. These girls were babies who should be with their mama, not here with us. I wanted to scream and cry—this was so unbearable. *Why, Lord? Why should they be put through all of this? Why are innocent children treated so badly?*

Then the thought came to me—these girls were the fortunate ones. They were getting a chance to escape.

After running the water, I washed and tried to soothe them. I want you to understand how terrified these kids must have been. I was a safe person, but they didn't know that. What did they think about this woman, a complete stranger, asking them to take off their clothes?

Although Elaine didn't take her eyes off her baby sister and watched every move I made, she was compliant and did everything I asked.

I wrestled with God. *Lord,* I prayed silently, *I can't do this task. I can't bear this load any longer. My heart can't take it. I'm too old for this.* Every part of me wanted to get out of the bathroom and run far away. Couldn't God find someone else to do this job? *Please, Lord, fill me up. Take my burden and carry it.*

Then I looked at Elaine. She had tears rolling down her face but said nothing as she reached over to help me wash the baby. I knew then I was doing what I needed to do and God would give me the strength to do it.

Elaine had the most stunning big brown eyes and rosy cheeks I had ever seen. Her lips seemed like they were perfectly sculpted and then painted a delicate shade of red. She looked like a porcelain doll that had been mistreated. It took only a moment to see that Elaine was tough and definitely in charge. She was only five, yet she seemed to have the weight of her sisters on her shoulders.

Evelyn, the middle girl, looked completely different from Elaine. She was dark haired and tall, quite striking with perfectly arched eyebrows and full pink lips.

The baby, Rose, on the other hand, was limp. Her eyes were empty like there was no life inside her.

Out of nowhere Evelyn began a high-pitched squeal, a sound that could shatter glass and peel the wallpaper right off the walls. It was so bad that Elaine broke her silence, turned around, and snapped, "Would you shut up! Just do what she says."

Evelyn immediately stopped her squealing and did what I asked her to do.

I chuckled inside and hoped they didn't notice my smile. I knew I needed to win Elaine over because she was clearly in charge.

Their hair was so tangled I had a tough time trying to wash it, and I couldn't get a comb through it, much less get all the lice out. I gave up trying, and after drying the girls off, I put clean clothes on them.

I got the social worker's permission to cut their hair, then took them to the garage, giving them each a bob cut. I felt bad but didn't see any other way. When I was done, three absolutely stunning girls had emerged.

George came up and said, "Come on, girls, let's go play on the trampoline." And off the two older girls went while I put the baby to bed.

Raymond and Samantha's story

Emotionally and physically weary, I went to sit down to talk with Domingo and the social worker. After we'd been officially introduced, she pointed to Samantha and Raymond. "Are those the Ross kids?"

"Yes," we said.

"Those poor children." She shook her head. Then, seeing the blank looks on our faces, she said, "Don't you know what happened to them?"

"We're waiting to find out," Domingo said. "Do you know?"

She took a deep breath and fingered the mug of tea Domingo had gotten for her. "Okay, here's what I know. We got a call about a family who lives up in the hills on a piece of property with several trailers on it. The property belongs to the grandmother of these kids. It's a filthy place. Stuff everywhere. There was a meth raid, and the sheriff's office called social services to come. It was very cold, in the twenties, and had snowed. We went into the trailer home, and the girl had on little clothing and was filthy. Mom fought the cop and got really mouthy, so they handcuffed her and put her in the patrol car. I took Samantha and put her in the social services car. The poor little girl started crying hysterically for her mom. We looked around but didn't see the little guy.

"'Where's the boy?' someone asked.

"'He's not here,' the mom said with an attitude. 'He's with family and friends.'

"'Are you sure?'

"Mom cussed everyone out, Samantha screamed louder, and everyone was ready to go. Except for Sheriff Bender. He wasn't getting in his car. He kept scanning the area; you could tell he was uneasy. Then he said, 'I have to go check the grounds one more time.'

"He looked around the property and found an old camper sitting on cinder blocks in a secluded area. As he got closer, he could smell the stench of feces and rotten food. He opened the camper door, and the stench blasted him. A toilet overflowed with excrement. Open cans of rotten food sat on the counter, garbage was strewn about, and animal feces were everywhere. In a corner he saw hundreds of flies. As he got closer, he saw a child lying there in the frigid temperatures, completely still, with nothing on but a soiled diaper. A baby bottle filled with rotten milk lay next to him. The baby's eyes were open but not registering anything. Because of all the flies swirling around him and landing on him, the sheriff thought the baby was dead.

"We all heard him calling for help, and those who could went running. I had to stay with Samantha. Pretty soon an ambulance arrived to take the baby to the hospital. The sheriff was so angry, they had to restrain him from laying into the mother.

"They think the family knew the baby was in the camper and planned to send someone back to get him later. I wonder, though. Would they have even remembered? How long had he been there before the sheriff found him? I shudder to think of what those kids endured living there."

After we heard the story, we understood what had caused the boils and why Raymond was angry much of the time. His anger demonstrated his strong will. I thanked God for it, believing that's what had kept him alive. And I fully believe this little guy would have died if it hadn't been for the sheriff. I was told the man was a Christian—and that something in his spirit had urged him to keep looking.

the girls' story

We had barely finished hearing Raymond and Samantha's devastating story when the social worker began to tell us what she knew about the girls I'd just bathed. My heart feared the truth about the extent of their pain—truth that would emerge slowly over the next months.

It had been 105 degrees in the city, and the girls were walking in the streets with their mother, barefoot and without access to food or water. Their mother was on meth, confused, dazed, paranoid, and not making much sense. She told her girls Grandma was poisoning them at home and they needed to get out. So they wandered. Their feet were black and sore, their tummies empty, their bodies dehydrated. At some point, while holding the baby, their mother pulled out her knife and tried to enter a car with people in it. Somehow the plan was thwarted, and the police came to handcuff her and take her away in a patrol car. The girls were put in a different patrol car and taken to the police station.

At the station, they put the girls and their mother together in a room with a video camera. The camera recorded Mom saying spine-chilling things to those little girls. "You'd better be careful," she warned. "They're going to take you away and put you with bad people. They're going to torture you and kill you."

The poor little girls were so terrified, they screamed and cried hysterically, "No! No!"

And then the social worker came and took them away.

"he will be yours"

I'm thankful that the girls came when they did and that I had to invest my time in them for a week, even though it was right in the middle of Samantha's crisis. If they hadn't been there, I would have obsessed about Samantha far more than would have been healthy for either of us. One reason we had to shift focus was because the baby, Rose, tested positive for meth. No wonder she had been so out of it! As she started going through withdrawals, she came alive—crazy alive. We had to walk the floor at night, holding her while she screamed. One night her breathing slowed so much, we almost took her to the ER, worried she might die. Whenever Domingo was home, he walked with her, never letting her out of his sight.

One day he looked at me while I was cuddling and rocking Raymond, and he said, "You're going to spoil that boy, Irene."

I laughed. "Look at you with that little girl! You're just as bad as I am."

The other two girls were crazy like little wildcats; Evelyn unnerved us all as she squealed for hours. The battle for Kurt was ongoing. We were fighting against visitation, and we wanted the father to be investigated for his abuse. Thankfully, George was doing well. Despite his family growing from one to six kids in a matter of months, he welcomed all his new siblings with an eagerness as well as tenderness. For years he had prayed earnestly for brothers and sisters, and these kids were God's answers.

It wasn't easy dealing with Samantha and Raymond's visits with their mom after their traumatic Memorial Day weekend. She was still allowed one visit per week, but now the visits were supervised. It took days to get the kids back to normal, and since they saw their mom every week, "normal" didn't happen very often. Samantha became clingy, and Raymond started his tantrums all over again, throwing himself on the floor, hitting his head hard on the tile. He frightened me. I thought he would crack his head in. Social services informed us that the paperwork was already in motion for their dad, who was being released from prison soon, to get full custody of the kids.

I couldn't believe the system. No matter what the parents did, the system almost always leaned toward reunification. Even meth-addicted parents could get their kids back after six months if they followed the requirements the court placed on them.

We later learned that Raymond also had a horrific experience Memorial Day weekend. He came close to death, again, when he slipped into a river and was drowning. A young man saw him and ran over to pull him out of the river. It doesn't surprise me that this little guy was not being supervised. So in one weekend, Samantha was abused and Raymond almost drowned. You can see why we were so upset at the thought of these kids going home with either parent.

One night I was so distraught over this, I couldn't sleep, so I went and got Raymond and brought him to the rocking chair in our bedroom. I held him and cried. I was so angry at God. I kept asking, "Why, God? Why would you let these precious children go back to such a dangerous place?" God had turned the ugly little baby into a beautiful toddler with golden hair and big brown eyes. As I looked at his sweet, relaxed face as he slept, I realized I had fallen in love with this boy and wanted to protect him. But here I was, on the verge of having to give him and his sister back.

When I slowed my anger, God whispered in my ear, "Have faith, Irene. This boy is not going back. He will be yours."

Peace filled me, and I put Raymond back in his crib. I went to bed and told Domingo what I'd heard, and he said, "You need to have faith, Irene, and believe what you heard."

The court charged their mom with child endangerment. She skipped bail and disappeared, turning up on the FBI's wanted list. Their dad came for his visit and brought Raymond a toy guitar and Samantha a toy piano. The visit seemed to go all right—and then no one ever saw him again.

girls

When the girls came, Samantha was excited to have sisters to share a room and play with. Elaine, in her self-assigned role as mother to all the little girls, immediately embraced Samantha, while Evelyn just put up with her.

Elaine and Evelyn seemed to be adjusting to their new environment. But they never asked about their mom, nor did they want to see her. This seemed peculiar to me. Most kids ask about Mom and Dad right away and would climb the highest mountain to visit their mom. Not these girls. They didn't even like to say their mom's name.

Although the baby started going through withdrawals and we couldn't comfort her, we were happy that she had begun showing emotions after the flat personality she had come with. It killed us that this little one had meth in her system. At a seminar on meth we had learned that the addiction is powerful and difficult to cure. Once you've taken meth, your body is forever changed. I couldn't fathom how a little baby was supposed to deal with this.

My anger started to grow until I hated their mom. Surely God didn't want me to love the parents who had hurt the children he had placed in my care!

It came as a relief when we learned their mom would be put away for a long time. She and a friend had snatched a toddler when she was a young teen high on meth. When the sheriffs arrived, the accomplice threw the child out the window. So the mom had served over a ten-year sentence before marrying the girls' dad. As a result of the prior conviction, the worker believed that these girls could be long-term in our home and then would shortly be moved into the foster-adoption program.

"Domingo," I said to him that night after we'd gotten all the kids to bed, "I think we should adopt these girls."

He said, "We can't adopt every child who comes our way."

"I know, Mingo. But these little girls …"

"I remember sitting in the agency office a little over a year ago, where you insisted you only wanted short-term kids. You did *not* want to adopt under any circumstance. That's not what we're here for, you said."

"Well, maybe I was wrong."

"You seem to forget—we're over fifty. And if we adopt, we won't be able to help very many kids. Isn't that what we came here for? To help kids be reunified with their parents?"

I knew he was right, but it was still hard for me to let go.

jail visit

Elaine *hated* her mom and was afraid of her at the same time. And while Elaine wanted nothing to do with her, Evelyn did—but only for the presents she figured her mom would bring her. She didn't want to stay with her mom; she only wanted the goodies.

I will admit, I admired their mom's persistence. She managed to get a judge to give her a visit with the girls. The only problem was, it had to take place in jail. The day I got the call, my world stopped. My heart was beating fast, my hand shaking as a storm brewed inside me. I felt contempt and a crazy sort of frenzy. What could I do? How could I stop this? I went and told Domingo, and I could tell he was sickened as well. We knew Elaine wouldn't be able to handle a visit with her mother—especially one in jail. We figured Evelyn would cope somehow, but we both felt Elaine would break. We prayed and begged God to cancel the visit, but to my disappointment that didn't happen.

The girls had just started opening up. They were smiling. And now we were going to make them visit their mother? When we told the girls, Elaine threatened to run away, and Evelyn cried.

The social worker had been fighting very hard for the girls and knew that a visit like this would be detrimental. The court order had tied her hands as well. Knowing how much the social worker cared for these girls helped a lot. And she promised she would stay with them the entire time.

I visited someone in prison once. The experience was frightening. Each time a door clanged shut behind me, I could feel a rumble and stirring in my bowels. How would these little girls feel each time a door was closed behind them?

That morning my husband and I reluctantly handed the crying, frightened girls over to the social worker. Then we went inside to pray and fast. Domingo grabbed my hand. "Irene. These are God's children, not ours. He will protect them."

Later that day, we heard the car pull up with the girls and ran outside to greet them. By the look on the social worker's face, I knew things had not gone well. Elaine bolted out of the car and ran straight to her room. Evelyn jabbered on about the jail and the food and gifts she got. Sisters—the same blood, yet so different. One let out too much, and the other held everything back.

The social worker came with me into the house. Once we got Evelyn settled in another room, playing with the other kids, the social worker was able to tell me what had happened.

Elaine had held on to the social worker with all her might, shaking and trembling like a little leaf the entire time. She put her head down, refusing to look at her mom. All Evelyn did was nervously talk about the snacks their mom gave them and play with the gifts.

The social worker was not happy about the visit and the effect on the girls. "I'm going to make sure these girls never have to go through this again," she told me. She kept her word and fought hard on behalf of the girls. When the courts understood their fearful experience, they did not require the girls to go to the jail for another visit.

dealing with the girls' behavior

Since Raymond and Rose were close in age, I'd put them together in a play area with toys in front of each of them. It didn't matter what Rose had, she wanted Raymond's toys. He let her take things from him and picked up a different toy to play with. Over and over he'd relinquish what he had so she could have it. And yet he had a special connection with her. He always watched out for her. Rose was so messed up, but he brought life to her and helped her heal. With his sweet little hands he patted her softly and said, "It's 'k, Rose." For a long time those were his only words. Who would've thought my little thug would have such a tender heart?

The big girls seemed to be adjusting overall, but they had a meanness about them that worried me. Elaine did all the right things in front of us. She helped out with everything—especially the baby. Like the others, she idolized George and followed him around. She was kind and good to the other kids, playing with Samantha and the babies. But the sad thing was, she didn't like Evelyn, and she made that obvious with her actions. She stole Evelyn's clothes, hid them, and threw them away. She took Evelyn's toys and broke them. She'd look at her sister with disgust and say, "I hate you." I asked her why she told Evelyn she hated her, and she said, "My mom made her an egg sandwich and bought her a balloon for her birthday, and she never did anything for me."

Having experienced a similar situation in my childhood, I told her, "I understand how you feel, Elaine, but you need to love your sister."

She began to cry, then walked away.

Evelyn was no saint. This girl could spew the most wicked and vile things back at her sister. She used words you might hear grown men say in anger. I would stare, astonished. How could such ugly words come out of such beautiful lips?

It seemed as though I never got off my knees for very long before I had to go back to God for more wisdom. "Lord, help," I prayed. "Show me how to handle these girls. You created them and you brought them to us. Please teach me how to care for them and train them."

Once when Evelyn was spewing vicious words, I told her she'd lost all but two hundred of her words for the rest of the day. The next day, she'd be allowed five hundred words. For every mean word she spoke, I would take away twenty-five from her "allowance." If she didn't use all her words for the day, she could save them in her "bank" and use them for the next day. She wanted to collect her words in her bank, so she tried to save as many as she could. She was so busy counting her words and saving them that she started to learn how to guard her tongue.

We also noticed odd behavior in Evelyn. She was always talking to someone who wasn't there. One afternoon I listened by her bedroom door and realized she was talking to a girl in a cage. She opened the cage to let her out, talked to her, then put her back in and locked the cage. She seemed to spend more time in this fantasy world than in our real world. All she wanted to do was go upstairs and play with the girl in the cage. I understood vivid imaginations. After all, I was a dreamer as a child. And I still talk out loud to myself and God. However, I would be setting the girl in the cage free, not locking her up.

As time went on, I realized that when things got tough and Evelyn didn't want to cope, she retreated to a make-believe world. She was (and still is) very creative and has a fascinating imagination. I didn't mind the imagination, just that it was very dark. She has said no one has hurt her. Knowing Evelyn, I think she would have told me if someone had. I think her dark, strange behavior grew out of the craziness in her home.

If she didn't want to obey, she could throw a mighty fit of rage. These fits were pretty daunting. She stomped her feet, shook her hands, rolled her eyes back in her head, and let out a high-pitched squealing cry. The tantrum could last for hours. Nothing worked to calm her, and none of us could handle it, so we gave her the downstairs bathroom as her own private rage space. We told her she could come back upstairs and join the rest of the family when she was done squealing. At first it terrified the other kids, and they got panicky when they heard her. Over time, though, the kids just stopped momentarily before saying, "It's only Evelyn." We believe those tantrums are why she can now sing so well and hold a note so long. She had a lot of practice exercising her vocal cords!

Rose's story

It was a lazy Saturday. Domingo had taken all the boys off to do boy things. I walked into the living room to find Evelyn doing something odd to Rose. She was taking her legs and holding them behind her. Elaine was looking closely and trying to help.

I looked at them a moment, then said, "What are you guys doing?"

"We're trying to figure out how Grandma and Greg tied Rose up," Evelyn said.

"What are you talking about?" My heart began to beat a little harder.

And they began to share their story.

One night their mom came home high and fell asleep on the sofa. The girls had not been alone. When their mother's husband, Rose's father, was taken to prison, she moved them all in with their grandmother and a man named Greg—both meth users.

Some time after their mom had fallen asleep, they could hear Rose screaming in the bathroom.

Elaine ran to her mother and shook her. "Wake up, Mom, wake up!" Mom didn't wake up, so Elaine shook her harder, screaming, "Please, Mom, get up—Mom, please! It's Rose!" Her mother still didn't wake up.

Elaine and Evelyn ran to the bathroom, and through the door they could see Rose undressed, her hands and feet tied behind her back. The man held her, and Grandma was doing something to her. "She was giving her medicine, I think," Elaine said. Elaine got so mad and tried to wake her mother again.

I'm not sure what happened next. But their mom eventually woke up. And when she found out what had happened, she knifed Greg, but not so badly that he needed serious medical care. After a few days, they were getting high together again. I was later told this man was a registered sex offender under Megan's Law.

We now understood why Rose had the physical problems she did. We understood why Elaine was so angry at her mom. We still didn't know how Rose got meth in her system. Was that the "medicine" Grandma was giving her that night? Or had she picked it up from residue?

This revelation of Rose's abuse was a rude awakening for us. The baby was only sixteen months old. Think how much she must have suffered!

As more stories began to tumble out, we learned that Elaine cooked and cared for the other girls because their mother did not. Elaine was the mama and still only a baby herself.

There was no longer a question about what our next steps would be. Domingo and I knew what we had to do. How could we be called Christians and not help the helpless? From this point on we would fight hard to protect these girls God had plucked out of their misery.

chapter 16

provision

home addition

The year 2006 started out reasonably calm. At least as calm as a family can be with seven children in various stages of health, adoption, visitations, and counseling. And, at this point, our home was bursting at the seams. Our sleeping arrangements were fine with us but not with the county. Raymond stayed in our room; Esther and Rose slept in the loft; George shared a room with Kurt; and Samantha, Evelyn, and Elaine were in one room. Soon Raymond would be three years old, and Rose would be right behind him, turning three a couple of months later. The law stated that once children turned three, they could no longer sleep in the same room as an adult. Where would we put them? There were supposed to be only two children to a room, and since we already had three girls in the one room, we simply couldn't put Rose in there. In order to keep all the children we had, we needed more space. The county had made many exceptions on our behalf, but we had reached the end of its generosity. It gave us

197

one year to increase the size of our house to comply with the requirements for foster homes, or we would have to give back two of the
kids.

From the beginning, we'd planned to expand the house, but
we ran into an unexpected financial roadblock and didn't have
the funds to build the addition we needed. Defeated, I asked God
why he would bring us this far and then expect us to decide which
kids to give back. I couldn't understand what God was trying to
teach us.

One day I was sitting in a parking lot, talking to a social worker
on the phone about the possibility of losing two of our kids, when
I looked up and saw a small sign with the name of a construction
company on it in a building window. The size and placement of the
sign seemed odd. I thought, *God, are you telling me something?*

As I always did when I felt prompted, I prayed. *Lord, can you
somehow use this company to show us how we can build an addition
with the money we have in our savings? I know we don't have enough
… but you spoke the universe into existence. This is an easy task for you,
Lord. I will not be anxious but will wait on you.*

God had brought us to a new place, given us jobs, and brought
us children, and now I had to wait and believe he would give us
more space. I would like to say I was confident, but I must confess
I felt more like Gideon—nervous and uncertain about how to pray.
So I kept praying the same prayer, adding a different twist to it each
time.

After many months had gone by, we were asked to share our
story at church. As I told my part of our story, I mentioned that we
needed more room for our children and I was waiting on God to

show us what we needed to do. Then Domingo got up and shared his conviction that we (as a church) need to start taking care of the orphans in our own community before we go to other countries to adopt children.

Some time later, my husband got a call from a man named Greg Bolin, who was the head of the men's ministry at our church. Apparently he had wanted to start a building ministry. The leadership team wanted to do something that gave men the ability to use their God-given talents, but they didn't know what that looked like. Greg remembered our testimony when he saw Domingo walking in front of him in the church courtyard, and God made it evident that he needed to approach Domingo and ask him what kind of help we needed. So this kind man called Domingo, and they met for lunch. Greg shared his idea about getting the guys in our church to help us build an addition. When Domingo came home he told me the story. "They'll take care of all the labor. But there's one catch—we'll have to pay for parts and supplies."

"How much would that cost us?"

Domingo laughed. "Exactly what we have in the bank."

"Who is this guy?"

Then he told me the name of the construction company. I couldn't believe it. I had no idea the owners went to our church. "Domingo, I've been praying specifically for this company to help us in some way with the addition."

It was an unbelievable time as the men broke ground and got busy working on this project. We were pretty new in the church, so it was mind-boggling that they would help us. It took a little over six months for them to add the twelve hundred square feet we needed.

Not long ago I was talking with Greg and told him about the prayer I had prayed in the parking lot when I looked up and saw his company's sign.

Greg looked puzzled. "What sign did you see?"

"A small sign in your office window."

He looked even more confused. "We didn't have any signs in the window."

I described the sign and placement of it.

A light seemed to go on behind his eyes. "Oh. I remember that sign. UPS was having a hard time finding us, so we put it in the window for a few days until we were sure they wouldn't have any more trouble."

I marvel at this whole sequence of events. What were the odds that I would be in that parking lot to see that sign in the few days it was in the window? Or that the owner would hear Domingo and me speak and then see Domingo right when he was wondering what the men's ministry should do?

We will be eternally grateful to all the men who labored so sacrificially, giving of their time, energy, and money to help us build the addition. God used these obedient and selfless people to do his work. Because of them, we were able to keep the children we had and make room to take in more if that's what God wanted.

Before I ever started praying, God knew what he was going to do. But he urged me to pray so I would pay attention and see what he did on our behalf. Now when the Holy Spirit nudges me to pray for something, no matter how silly, impossible, or out of our reach it might seem, I just do it. I want to see God move mountains ... because he can ... and he does.

the girls' dad

Our social worker called to tell me Elaine and Evelyn's dad had contacted her office. He had been in jail for a while and had recently been released and wanted to see his girls. Elaine and Evelyn's parents had met in juvenile hall when they were young. Dad was in a gang and had taken the life of a gang rival. Mom was there because of the charges of kidnapping and child endangerment. Both Mom and Dad were adults when they got out.

Elaine and Evelyn didn't remember their dad. Apparently their mom took off with the kids when they were only three and two and wouldn't let their father see them. By now it had been about five years since they'd seen him, so they really had no memories of him. But because of how things work in the foster care system, they didn't have a choice. Elaine was adamant about not going. Someone told Evelyn he had gifts for them. She didn't want to see him but asked if he could send them the gifts.

The girls were afraid to go on the visit with their dad, but it wasn't like the fear of visiting their mom in jail. It was the fear of visiting a virtual stranger that unnerved them. Fortunately the first visit had been scheduled to take place at the agency, a place that was familiar to them.

Dad kindly called to talk to them on the phone beforehand, hoping that would soften the blow. I spoke to him before handing the receiver to the girls, and he seemed truly kind and gentle. Their first visit was reasonably successful. Nothing horrible happened. It was just uncomfortable for all of them. It was clear Elaine still didn't want anything to do with her dad, and although Evelyn liked his attention, she pursed her lips and acted really shy and sheepish.

As the visits continued, Dad began to bring his girlfriend—who the kids knew through their mother—on the visits. He didn't have restrictions for supervised visitation like their mom had, so when he came to town, he was able to do fun things with the girls. That didn't matter to Elaine. She wanted to stay home. Evelyn was fine until she found out she might have to live with them; after that she didn't want any more visits.

the first Garcias

In October 2006, we celebrated our first finalized adoption by going to Denny's. That's what the kids wanted, so off we went with the gang. Although we'd started Kurt's process first, Samantha and Raymond became the first official Garcias. Their adoption was easy and quick. So much for getting "short-term only" kids and not getting attached! I think God just smiles at our plans, knowing he's going to change them anyway—along with our hearts.

One morning, not long after Samantha's and Raymond's adoptions were final, I came into the living room to see Samantha wearing a crown on her head, walking regally down the stairs. Elaine and Evelyn were walking behind her, holding a make-believe train. "This is Queen Samantha!" they said as they continued their ceremony. "She is a queen because now she is a *real* Garcia. She *belongs*."

Until then I hadn't realized how badly the girls wanted to be adopted, to belong and be a part of our family. I know this might sound weird, but it made me think about our place as children of God. When God adopts us, we are heirs with Christ and become kings and queens. Now whenever I think about being heirs with

Christ, I see Samantha with her crown, floating down the stairs.
How special we are to God!

the van—2007

One of the county's requirements was that we needed to have
a vehicle large enough to fit all of us at the same time. With our
growing family, that meant we needed a large vehicle, preferably a
fifteen-passenger van. We'd used all our money on the addition, so
we figured we'd buy a used van on credit.

God had shown us he was faithful and would provide for all of
our needs, and this certainly qualified. We began praying for a van,
fully believing that God would provide one, but thought it might
take a while. As we started looking, we saw that used vans—especially
ones the size we needed—were quite expensive, which reinforced the
reality that we would have to finance one.

As I prayed, the thought came to me that maybe instead of
financing a van through the bank, we should increase our tithing,
giving the money to God instead. I know that doesn't make sense to
most people. Thankfully, Domingo got it. When I shared my convictions with him, he said, "Let's do it." So we increased the amount of
our tithe to what a van payment would be. I was so excited. I was
really going to trust God for this van.

Then I found the perfect one. It was a year old with only eleven
thousand miles on it and reasonably priced. It was like new and the
deal of a lifetime—but we still didn't have the money.

My faith faltered like doubting Thomas. I kept thinking we
would never find another one as good, so maybe we should go ahead

and finance it. In my struggle, I knew I could either get a van my way … or I could trust God. I wanted to trust, so I put the van out of my mind.

A few days later our accountant called to tell us we were getting a substantial amount of money back from our income taxes. When we sold our business, we'd overpaid the taxes. Of course—it was the exact amount we needed for the van.

By the time the men had completed our addition, we also had a fifteen-passenger van. So God supplied the space and a van, and now all we needed was the kids to complete our family.

The girls had been with us over a year. Rose was regularly visiting her parents, who had reconciled. Raymond's and Samantha's adoptions gave them stability. The tough little Chicken Hawk now belonged to us. No longer Mama's boy, he was attached to his new dad, following him everywhere. The battle for Kurt seemed never ending, but at least he was with us and doing very well physically and mentally. Steady George loved being a big brother and played his role so well.

Elaine and Evelyn didn't have visits with their mom but did have regular visits with their dad. I was so brokenhearted. It looked like he was going to get custody of them. The girls loved us and their new home. For the first time in their lives they were feeling the stability of a family and were growing in leaps and bounds. They had started calling us Mom and Dad and begged us not to let them be taken away. They were so anxious and distraught they couldn't sleep.

We had met Elaine and Evelyn's dad and talked to him on the phone weekly. He had made some real changes in his life, including attending all the classes that were required of him. He knew how we felt about the girls and how they felt about us. He was kind and thanked us for taking good care of his girls. And although he was trying to win their affection, the girls didn't know him and didn't really want to.

During one conversation, he shared a lot about his past and his regrets about his life. He told us he was a Christian now and had given his life to God.

I asked him if he would consider letting us have the girls, and he said he'd never stop fighting for them. We explained they had a lot of needs that included therapy and encouraged him to think about what was best for them—and reminded him that separating them from Rose would be detrimental.

A few weeks later he was coming to town for court, and he agreed to meet Domingo for dinner at a restaurant. As they talked, he continually blamed his ex-wife for the suffering of his girls. Then Domingo boldly asked him, "Where were you when they were picked up with their mom?"

He hesitated. "In jail."

"Well, you weren't there for them," Domingo said. "They needed you, and you weren't there. Their situation is as much your fault as their mom's."

The man's face displayed a battle of emotions. Anger, maybe shock, sadness.

Domingo continued, "I only care about what's best for the girls and what God wants for them."

The man leaned forward. "I'm not going to give up my girls. I will fight for them until the end."

"How can you give them the special care they need?" Domingo asked.

"My girlfriend will help."

"I tell you what. Go home and pray about it. And I will too."

I had been praying for their meeting to go well. As I prayed, I felt we needed to let the dad come to our home and see the girls in their environment. Just then Domingo called. "Irene, how do you feel about me inviting the girls' dad over? I believe it's our responsibility to show God's love to him, no matter what."

Sometimes showing God's love is scary for me. We didn't really know this man or what he might do once he knew where we lived. But I knew it was the right thing, so I agreed. A few weeks later we invited him and his girlfriend over for a barbecue. And the visit was good for all of us. I knew that this was God at work, changing my heart. I was always fearful of the parents of our kids, yet here I was inviting one over. *Wow.* I often forget the blessings I receive when I obey the prompting of the Spirit.

Kurt court

Kurt's visits with his parents didn't get any better. We saw the pain in his life and the disconnection from his parents. Every part of me wanted to bring this boy in and wrap him in the safety of a home with two parents who cared about him. Domingo had talked with George, and George certainly wanted Kurt to stay.

I must admit I had the attitude that I could do a better job with these kids than their parents. How arrogant is that? I had to continue to remind myself that I was a caretaker, not a parent. I was only a stand-in until the parents could get back on their feet. But what about when the parents didn't see they'd done anything wrong or harmful to their children? Should we hand the kids back over as though nothing had happened?

"Oh, Lord," I prayed, "show us what we need to do."

Adopting Kurt was a battle. It seemed like everywhere I turned, there was something I had to deal with. I tried to work with his social worker, but she was never around. She'd promise to come, then not show up. There was some glitch in the process, and his mom was given another six months to comply with the court order. I finally spoke to our social worker and asked her to help, and she got us a hearing before the judge.

The judge was not impressed with the mom. When he found out she had let Kurt's teeth rot, he lit into her. "Why did you not take him to the dentist?"

"Well," she started to explain, "I hate dentists and have a real fear of them. I didn't want him to go through the pain I did."

The judge fumed and rebuked her. "But you let him suffer the pain of rotten teeth? How is that better than going to a dentist?" It also came out that although Kurt had been enrolled in speech therapy, his mom never took him.

When the social worker asked Kurt what he wanted, he said he didn't want to go home with his parents. He told everyone who would listen that he hated them and wanted to be with us. One evening when it was Kurt's turn to pray before dinner, he prayed in his struggling but determined voice, "Please keep my dad in jail, and send my mom there too!" We about choked but then gently explained that some prayers need to be prayed in private.

Domingo and I try to teach these kids to honor their parents. It's tough, considering who the parents are and what they've done, but God doesn't make a distinction about which parents to honor. He just says, "Honor your father and mother." Period. One way we do that is to encourage the children to forgive their parents and pray for their salvation.

After a long fight, Kurt became ours in January 2007. He seemed to grow fearless overnight. He shone with an aura of self-assurance. He could pucker his lips at the slow drop of a hat. The diagnosis of intellectually disabled turned out to be wrong. He *is* autistic and has physical disabilities, but he's also intellectually smart—in fact, he's brilliant. This twelve-year-old boy reads at a high school level, writes well, and has a photographic memory. He is a walking encyclopedia.

As I watch Kurt play basketball, his feet and arms all going in different directions as he runs, I am reminded of the beauty of innocence. He has the biggest smile on his face and has no idea that he's different from the rest of the kids. But that's what makes him special.

There was a time when my heart would ache as I watched my disabled children trying to fit in with the kids around them. But now I praise God for my special blessings. Many might say a disabled child is God's mistake. But being a mother of many disabled kids, I can share that they are truly God's blessings, not his mistakes. I know that my children were perfectly created, because I know the hands of their Creator. Psalm 139:14–15 says, "I will give thanks to You, for I am fearfully and wonderfully made; wonderful are Your works, and my soul knows it very well. My frame was not hidden from You, when I was made in secret, and skillfully wrought in the depths of the earth" (NASB).

Each one of my children, no matter how different, was created for a purpose, and that purpose is to glorify our King.

chapter 17

Mac and Tony

Just a few months after Raymond's and Samantha's adoptions, and at the tail end of our fight for Kurt, Domingo called me at work to tell me that the agency had a short-term placement of a two-year-old boy who had overdosed on his mom's drugs. Well, we had our fifteen-passenger van and were just finishing the addition. Excitement filled my heart. God was filling our home.

When I got home, the kids raced up to me and spilled the information about this boy. They told me that the boy's name was Mac and that Domingo was giving him a bath. The girls chattered on about how cute he was, and the boys reported that he didn't sit up and play.

When I walked into the room, all I could think was, *That's a very big boy*. This boy was a chubba-wubba, weighing over forty pounds. I said hello to him, and he looked into my eyes with no expression— not even fear. This boy didn't know me, he had never been in our home, yet he sat in the tub expressionless. He reminded me of Rose when she had arrived with meth in her system.

A normal two-year-old in a strange environment will scream and cry for his mommy. Not only did this boy not make a sound, but when I reached out to take him from the bath, he didn't resist. I put my hands under his arms to pick him up and almost fell into the tub with him! He was so stinking heavy—he didn't put his legs around me or help in any way like a toddler usually does. He just hung there. The moment I had him in my arms, he dropped his gigantic head against my chest, knocking the air out of me. It felt as if someone had punched me as hard as they could.

Mac was a pretty easy child because he couldn't walk or even sit very well, so we didn't worry about him getting into trouble. We thought his poor motor skills were because of the drugs he had taken. We later found out that Mac's mom confined him in a really small space so he wouldn't move. Her reasoning was that she moved around a lot, so he needed to be caged in. This little baby had not experienced the freedom of walking and running.

His mom made sure Mac had plenty to eat. But it was usually Trix cereal or an extralarge pizza to share with his sister. It didn't take an intellect to figure out that this kind of food and no exercise makes for a big, big boy!

It was no easy task to get Mac walking. With all the girls oohing and gooing at him, he eventually got to his feet—but he wasn't very steady. Mac was wobbly on his feet for a really long time and needed to hold someone's hand.

When I picked him up, he still hung as though he had no muscle tone. We couldn't get him to talk, and he never cried. He could fall hard and we wouldn't hear a peep out of him. We'd find bruises and cuts on his body like you'd find on any normal toddler, but we had no idea when or how he got them since he didn't make a sound.

When I think of babies, I think, *Cry, eat, cry, change, cry.* The only time we saw any emotion from Mac was when I changed his diaper. He kicked, fought, hit, and let out skin-tingling wails. I am not a wimp and am very strong willed. But changing Mac's diaper was like wrestling an alligator. I'm no fool. I asked Domingo for help. Surprisingly, Mac let Domingo change him without a fight. It only made sense for Domingo to take over diapering Mac.

As time went on, it became obvious that Mac was mentally delayed as well as physically delayed. His mom had reported that he was a normal two-year-old who began walking at one. That didn't make sense based on what we saw. One afternoon I took him to his evaluation with his birth mom and a psychologist. His mom told us that Mac had climbed onto the counter, gotten her bag of drugs from a cabinet, and ate them. She said she called the paramedics right away. When the paramedics arrived, Mac wasn't breathing.

Something about the story didn't ring true to me.

After she told us her version of what happened, the psychologist gave the mom and me the same questionnaire to fill out separately. When we finished, she compared our answers. They were so different that it looked like we couldn't possibly be assessing the same child.

The mom sat there and looked at the psychologist and said emphatically, "Mac is a normal little boy. He did everything on schedule that he's supposed to." The psychologist nodded.

It was hard enough sitting in this room with a woman who had picked up her baby's arm while he was unconscious, let it drop like dead weight onto the table, and laughed in front of the paramedics.

But watching the psychologist agree with her that her kid was normal just about did me in. I was getting angrier by the minute. I wanted to shake them both and shout, "Wake up, you idiots! This boy is *not* normal. He can't talk, I have never heard him cry, and he still walks with sea legs." People say I'm such a patient woman. It's not true. I'm not patient; it's just that the Holy Spirit has taught me to keep my mouth shut! So instead of saying all the things I really wanted to, I settled for a controlled but firm "No way!"

The psychologist asked more questions and finally conceded that there was a strong possibility of brain damage because of the overdose.

Then it hit me—*bam!* Maybe he *had* been normal before this incident. And he'd still be normal if he'd not eaten his mother's drugs. This mother had abused her baby and felt no remorse over what she had caused. Instead, she was trying to make me look crazy and overzealous about this boy. The same emotions I'd had when I was told George had cancer swept through me, and my biggest enemy—fear—took command of every part of my being. The reality was that this boy could never be normal, and he was going to be our responsibility. Such information would put a normal person in shock, but I went into overload because of my fear. It was too much. Then I heard someone say, "Mrs. Garcia," and my mind returned to the room.

After much testing, Mac was diagnosed as intellectually disabled. This didn't surprise us at all. Another mystery was solved when the doctors told us he had a disease called pica. This meant he'd eat anything and everything. He ate Legos, cars, blocks, balls, and dirt. Once he could get around better he ate anything he could reach in the cupboards. We had to watch this boy like a hawk. It got to the point where we had to lock our pantry. It didn't matter to us that he *ate* food; the problem was that he *ate it all*. Whole loaves of bread, blocks of cheese, bags of chips. If someone had a snack hidden anywhere, believe me, he would find it and eat it.

We bought some open panels that could be turned into an extralarge playpen. We put his toys in it, and he would stay in there and play happily. When he started getting better at walking, Domingo took him wherever he went; all this boy wanted was to be with Domingo. He stuck like glue to Domingo's side and became very possessive, not wanting to share him with the other kids.

We were told that Mac was probably going back to his mom. I knew that Domingo, in his heart, wanted to adopt Mac. I wasn't so sure about adopting him. I kept thinking we might have only twenty years left if God was gracious. This boy needed young parents who would be around for a long time, which was something Domingo and I couldn't give.

March 2007

One night I was lying in bed, thinking. Even though Domingo really enjoyed Mac and Mac was attached to Domingo and learning so much from him, the little boy would be leaving soon. Without him, our family would feel incomplete. I woke Domingo and asked him how he'd feel about taking in a hard-to-place little boy, one no one else wanted. After all our years of marriage, he knew that when I felt something unusual and unexpected, something that made no sense, it had to be the Spirit. When the Spirit prompts, no matter how radical it seems, Domingo and I have learned to respond with *yes*. There are times things don't turn out the way we think they should. But even then we learn a valuable lesson that helps us later on in life. So when I woke him with this odd thought, his response was quick: "Let's do it." From that point on we began praying specifically for a hard-to-place little boy.

When I shared our desire with others, I knew they thought I was off my rocker. At times I felt that way too, but I also knew I had to trust the prompting of the Spirit no matter how kooky it seemed.

A few days after we told our social worker, we got a call about a little boy who had been in *seven* placements! He was ready and available now, which was not the norm. She said he had been in adoption placements twice, but both families backed out.

This was curious. When a child reaches a potential home, it's because the parents really want the child as their own, so they work hard to resolve issues. If *two* families had him in their homes with the commitment to adopt, and *both* backed out—I thought, *Whoa, we are on our way to a new and wild adventure.* What I didn't know was that the adventure would soon turn into a nightmare.

The social worker brought the boy over to meet us. Tony was pretty cute and had a great personality, dark skin, and big brown eyes. The thing that captured us from the first moment was his smile—it spread from ear to ear and lit up the room. To this day we refer to him as Smiley. No matter how bad things got, he would always smile. He would get in trouble and lie ... but still have this gigantic smile on his face.

Almost five-year-old Tony played with some toys in another room as the social worker proceeded to share his story. His birth mom drank and took drugs during her pregnancy. He was first taken away from her when he was about two. Then he was given back to his mom before being given to his grandma. Apparently his mom wanted him to grow up and be in a gang, so she beat him to make him tough.

The next six placements all gave their seven-day notices, which means, "I want this kid out of my house now!" The last family had him for a year. I wondered how someone could have a child for that long and not want to adopt him. I figured he was so out of control that no one wanted him. But maybe, I thought, no one wanted him because he really belonged to us. Somehow, in my crazy thinking, this helped soften the thought of such a cantankerous and defiant boy.

Smiley was a product of the system. He had a social worker who made excuses for him and blamed others for his bad behavior. He came to us a month shy of turning five. This boy thought that he could tell us all what to do and we would listen. He was mean, foul-mouthed, destructive, combative, quarrelsome, hot tempered, and sneaky; he kicked, hit, bit, stole, was abusive to animals, and was a skilled liar. The bottom line was, Smiley was angry. Not only had his mom rejected him, but so had seven other families. He was so angry he just wanted to hurt someone. He thought we wouldn't keep him either. So this boy did everything he could to sabotage his life with us. And even though all his bad behaviors were documented, nothing helped us when he lied about us.

Well, I had to admit, God had answered our prayers. He brought us a boy who was hard to place, a boy no one else wanted.

On Tony's fifth birthday he was officially placed in our home. We had presents waiting for him to celebrate his birthday. After he had been in our home for two weeks, he had already caused much chaos, division, and hurt to our family. We knew he was a gift from God, so we would not give up—though many times I admit the thought occurred to me that I should return this gift because it didn't fit and I really didn't like it at all!

"What were you thinking?" I said, upset. "Why did you hit your brother?"

He looked me square in the eyes and said in the sweetest voice, "I didn't hit him. What are you talking about?"

"I saw you hit him."

"No, I didn't," he said with a huge smile on his face.

A combination of disbelief, fury, and exasperation over not knowing what to do flooded me. So I did what most irrational people do—I started shouting at him.

The other kids all shouted at the same time: "Yes, you did." "He hit him, Mom."

Tony's smile stayed on his face as he said, as sweet as can be, "I didn't hit him. They're all lying."

I picked him up, carried him into the house, and sat him on a chair.

He glared at me and said, "I'm going to call my social worker."

"You're going to sit there and tell me the truth."

He refused to budge. There wasn't a whole lot I could do. The system really ties our hands as foster parents. As a consequence, we're allowed to give children one minute of time-out per year of age. Five minutes of time-out was nothing for this kid. He continued to lie and hit the other kids, so we had to separate him from them by keeping him by our sides. However, every time we gave him grace or trusted him, he would hurt one of the kids again. Man, this little boy was tough. As you can imagine, we were continually on our knees, asking for wisdom.

We really didn't want to say this, but we finally told our kids they could defend themselves if we weren't there. But they still needed to come and get us right away if there was a problem.

Shortly afterward the kids were outside playing, and Tony kicked Rose in the face. George immediately pushed him away from her. From then on, my kids stuck together and protected one another from him, defending themselves until we got there.

I knew God wouldn't give us more than we could handle, but it seemed like he was taking us to the point where we might break. We had to trust God for wisdom because we knew he wanted us to keep this boy.

One particularly tough time was when his social worker dropped in for a visit. All the social workers we had worked with before would call ahead of time to schedule their visits. So I was taken by surprise when this woman showed up. It was incredibly inconvenient because I had three appointments that day, including another worker coming over.

She shrugged. "I don't have to schedule an appointment to come visit my cases," she said in a tone that irritated me.

"That's fine, but I need to be leaving shortly," I told her. My tone wasn't much better than hers.

"I would like to meet with Tony alone, please."

I thought this was strange, but I showed her his room. They were inside for a long while. When she came out, she told me she knew this boy's family, that they were doing well and he should be with them. That didn't make sense because he'd been in adoptions for a long time, but I said nothing. I was glad when she left.

Sometime afterward our worker called and said she was coming over with Tony's worker. When they arrived, I knew something was wrong. They both went into the bedroom with him, and when they came out, I gave him a peanut butter sandwich for lunch. "I don't want it," he said. "I want some *taquitos* with *frijoles* and *chillito*." I laughed to myself and looked at his worker, thinking she would be smiling as well. Instead I detected anger.

She later rebuked us because we didn't give him what he wanted for lunch. Can you imagine what things would be like if we fed all the kids what they wanted? This is not a restaurant, and I don't know any households that cater to their kids like that.

Well, this boy and his worker were really testing my patience.

Another day my husband called me to the front door. A social worker was standing there, talking with him. My heart started beating really fast, and my stomach felt like it leaped into my mouth. I knew we were in trouble for something, but what? My mind raced as I tried to think what we could have done wrong now! Were they going to take my kids?

I lived with this fear all the time. I don't know why, but so many people wanted us to fail. I got so tired of parents, attorneys, and even some social workers who continually made allegations against us.

As we invited the social worker in, I asked God to protect us. I hated that I always felt so much fear about what was going to happen next. I'm always thinking the worst, and Domingo continually reminds me, "Trust God and do the right thing, and whatever happens will be God's will."

I wish I had the trust my husband has.

The social worker said Tony had apparently shared with his worker that our kids were mean to him, George hit him with a stick, I beat him, the kids ganged up on him, and we told our kids it was okay to hit him.

"There is some truth about the kids defending themselves," I told her. I thought it was funny—it was documented that this boy was a compulsive liar and mean to other kids, yet these people didn't seem to expect him to act that way with us. Domingo and I shared our side of the story.

After the social worker wrote some notes, she asked if she could meet with Tony and the other kids alone. One by one she met with each of the kids. Can you imagine how this terrified them? But it had to be done. After she was in the bedroom for a while, she came out with Tony. "So," she said, "I heard the boy had pizza and soda for breakfast this morning."

At the same moment, both my husband and I said, *"What?"*

The social worker winked at us and said, "Okay, Tony, go get the soda you had for breakfast from the refrigerator."

He went to the refrigerator and opened the door, but there was no soda. He looked at the worker and said, "Someone must have stole it."

We sat down again, and she told us he had these fascinating stories about all of us. Tony has the gift of gab and can make up some very believable stories. He told her how mean we all were and that he was even afraid of little Rose.

She said, "Well, Tony, do you want to leave?"

"No way!"

"But if they're so mean, why would you want to stay?"

He straightened, looked her right in the eye, and said, "Don't you know? We Garcias stick together."

After Tony went off to play, she told us she knew he had been lying and that's why she asked him what he had for breakfast. "If any of the stories he told me were true, he would have wanted to leave." She smiled. "But this boy definitely wants to stay, doesn't he?"

We all laughed. I laughed out of relief that his allegations were deemed false.

chapter 18

Ruth

Elaine and Evelyn were about to go on their first plane ride, and they weren't the least bit excited. The plan was for them to visit their dad and new stepmom in the southern part of the state for three days. "Mommy" Elaine had never been separated from her baby girl Rose. As Rose's protector, Elaine couldn't bear the thought of being away from her. This, combined with the thought of being separated from us, made her miserable. She went to her room and quietly cried.

Since she'd come to live with us, her big brown eyes had slowly taken on a shine and glow. But once this trip was planned, the light in her eyes started to dim, and she began to retreat inside herself again. There wasn't much we could do except reassure both her and Evelyn.

About a week before they left, I discovered I could attend a color workshop for hairstylists in the part of the state where they'd be with their father. I signed up and told the girls that as soon as their visit was over, I'd pick them up rather than having them fly home. I hoped this plan would alleviate their sadness and fears somewhat. And it did help. They were very excited I would be picking them up.

It was difficult to concentrate on my workshop. My mind was on the girls. I missed them so much and was anxious to hear how they were doing. I was so eager to see them that I arrived at the pickup spot early. I pictured them happy to see me, running to the car with their arms open. Instead, they were so quiet when they got out of their dad's car, I wondered if they might be upset with me. Instead of the joyful reunion I had imagined, it felt dreary, with something tense hanging in the air.

I encouraged the girls to wave at their father as we drove off. Instead, they cried and said they didn't want to go back. "Did something bad happen?" I asked, my heart in my throat as I thought about Samantha's visit.

"No," they said through their tears. Their dad had taken them out and really tried to show them a good time, but they just wanted to be home with us.

When we got home, I was surprised when they came out of their room with letters they had written to their attorney and judge, asking them to please not make them go to visitation anymore.

At the pickup, I sensed their dad's sadness and disappointment with how the time with his daughters had gone. Most parents don't understand. They come out of prison and expect to start where they left off when their kids were taken away. It's hard for them to understand that their kids have moved on, adapting to their new situation. Most kids will change after a few years, but parents still remember them the way they were and expect to go right back to how the relationship was. They forget they've missed so much of the child's life. So many of the small milestones that are crucial to a child's development.

welcoming Ruth

One morning when I was in the kitchen, I got a call from the county. It was unusual for the county to call me directly since it was protocol for it to call the agency we worked with and let them contact us.

The county worker told me she wanted to talk to me about taking in Mac's sister so they could be together. I knew he had a sister, but I didn't know anything else about her. I had no idea she was in a temporary shelter.

Tony had come to live with us just a month before, and believe me, he was out of control. Domingo and I had learned that every time we took in a new child, our household would be chaotic for about six months. I was afraid Tony would cause chaos for years. We were in over our heads with problems again.

When I told her I didn't know if we could handle Ruth, she became very persistent. Somehow she knew how we felt about Mac and threatened to take him out of our home.

We knew this wasn't an idle threat. It made sense that they would want to put both children in a home together. But Mac's leaving would be detrimental to him because of his attachment to Domingo. He was finally starting to respond to us, and he was getting comfortable with our routine.

This was one time we were not ready to take in another child. Mac was a handful, and we were having major problems—Elaine, Evelyn, and Rose's mom was causing issues both in and out of court, and Tony had the social worker at our home a lot because he kept lying about things she had to check out. We got on our knees, and yes, we pleaded for wisdom.

So many forks in the road, so many life-changing decisions needing to be made in an instant. "Oh, dear God," I pleaded, "I am your vessel for you to use, but sometimes I feel broken and in dire need of repair. Please, God, fill my cracks so I can be useful for your service. Give us the wisdom to make your decision, not ours."

I called the social worker to get more information, and she told me Ruth was a good girl and pretty normal for a child who had been in placement. She told me Ruth had done very well in the shelter. She also made it clear that if we said no, Mac would have to leave.

Domingo and I discussed it. Social workers are required to disclose all they know, and this one said Mac's sister was pretty normal. And there was a calmness about Mac, so we figured, how bad could she be? We agreed it would be best for Mac if we took her in too. I must confess that if I'd known what she was really like, I probably would have said no because we were already submerged under so many burdensome situations.

I went to pick up Ruth from the shelter, and four girls came out at the same time. There was an older girl and three younger girls. I knew Ruth was four, soon to be five, so I tried to figure out which one of these younger girls was Mac's sister. I picked the one who looked rather shy and timid like Mac. When I said hello, the older, bossier girl who seemed to be in charge was the one who gave all the girls a hug and then walked over to me. She was matter-of-fact and said, "I'm ready." She was very tall for her age—probably about a foot taller than her friends. Of course, I should have guessed she would be the biggest of the bunch.

Before we left, I spoke to the foster mom to get all the information I needed about Ruth. After giving me the usual types of basic information, she handed me a bottle of pills.

"What are these for?" I asked.

"To help her sleep. Just give her one at night."

This didn't sound right to me. Why would a child need sleeping pills? I figured I'd talk to her worker in the morning and get it all figured out.

When Ruth got into the car, I could see some resemblance to Mac. She wasn't the least bit shy and talked to me like she had known me for years. She asked about her brother, then she said, "Did you know he ate my mom's pills and almost died?"

I nearly choked.

Ruth proceeded to freely tell me her version of the story—and it didn't quite line up with her mother's version.

Mom had blocked Mac in a very small area between the sofa and coffee table and chairs—which she did frequently so he wouldn't get into mischief or get in her way. He didn't have room to do anything but sit. She left her drugs within reaching distance on the coffee table in a plastic bag. Ruth came into the room and saw him eating them from the bag. She told him to stop, and he passed out. Ruth tried to wake up her mom, but she wouldn't wake up. Some man who was there called the ambulance. Paramedics performed CPR. Then, Ruth remembers, the police came.

"I thought he was going to die," she said between her tears. "I was so scared." She was only four. I can't even grasp what she went through that night.

Her story coincided with what the psychologist had told me— that Mac had stopped breathing and for a time had no oxygen to his brain, which most likely caused brain damage. Ruth told me he had never walked and didn't know how to talk. Her story made me believe that he was delayed before he ate the drugs and that the overdose made it all worse.

As I pulled into my driveway, all four of my girls were there, waiting to check Ruth out. The moment Ruth got out of the car, the girls took ownership of their home.

It was pretty funny to watch. Elaine laid some ground rules, and Evelyn told Ruth they were not allowed to wear heels, so she hoped she had some real shoes instead of the heels she had on. They continued to lay down the law, doing my job to make sure she knew what was appropriate in the Garcia household. I wasn't sure if they were being cautious or jealous.

I could tell Ruth was used to being in charge and getting her way. She had a real sweet attitude, but it wasn't sincere. It was so fake I wondered if she really believed I would fall for it. *So young and already scheming. Oh my*, I thought, *I'm in for it—my days are numbered.* I was definitely on a battlefield. One big problem—I didn't know anything about the enemy!

Since we really didn't have much information on her, we had to be careful and watch out for our younger kids. It's a sad thing, but most girls who come into the foster system have either been molested or been around sexually inappropriate behavior. So for this reason we put her in our daughter Elaine's room. Believe me, Elaine would watch Ruth like a hawk.

We really wanted to know more about Ruth, but her social worker hadn't returned my call.

That night after I put her to bed, I heard her crying.

I went into her room and sat on the edge of her bed. "What's wrong?"

"I hear voices in my head, and they won't stop."

"What kind of voices?" I pushed the hair off her forehead.

"Scary ones. They talk to me at night and tell me to do bad things. I'm so scared."

"Do you know who Jesus is?"

"I think so." She told me she'd gone to church with someone, so she had heard his name before.

"Well, Jesus died on the cross for all of us. When he lives in our hearts we are never alone and don't need to be afraid. He is always there to protect you."

"I want Jesus," she said, sitting up in bed. "I don't want to be afraid and hear scary people talk to me at night. Please help me make those scary people go away." What she said next broke my heart. "Will Jesus take care of me and Mac and feed us?"

I explained that Jesus would use Domingo and me to be his hands and feet. So we would make sure they would eat and be taken care of. "Do you want Jesus to live in your heart?"

"Yes," she said, her voice quiet but confident.

I knelt beside her bed and held her hand, and we prayed. When we opened our eyes, I tucked her in a little more snugly. "Anytime you're afraid, pray to Jesus. Now that he's in your heart, Jesus will protect you. Ask Jesus to take away the bad voices, and he will."

Later that night when I checked on her, she was sound asleep.

A few weeks after her arrival, I got a call from the health nurse asking me if I was giving Ruth her meds.

"What meds? All I have are sleeping pills."

The nurse became angry and short with me. "It's very important that you give her the meds."

I was frustrated. I'd tried to reach the social worker without success, and the foster mother had given me little information. "This isn't my fault. No one told me she had meds besides the sleeping pills."

"This girl is under psychiatric care. Her prescriptions are critical for her mental health."

"That's fine," I said, my own anger growing. "But I am not giving her any medication until I talk to the doctor."

The woman's voice rose, and she threatened to have Ruth taken out of our home.

"Go ahead," I said. "Come and get her. I will not give any child medication unless I know what it's for and am given instructions by a doctor." I could hear the boys starting to squabble over a toy in the next room. That did not help my mood any. "It's a big liability to give a child medication when I don't understand what it's for." What I didn't say, and wanted to, was that clearly since a few weeks had gone by and the girl was okay, it wasn't like life or death if she wasn't medicated. "Look. I promise I'll make an appointment with the doctor as soon as we hang up."

She curtly ended the conversation, probably as unhappy with me as I was with her. I kept my promise and called the doctor immediately, taking the first available appointment. I hung up, glad we would soon learn more about Ruth.

As Ruth became more comfortable in our surroundings, she was no longer the sweetheart she portrayed herself to be in the first few days and started bucking every rule. She was strong willed and would throw these unbelievable tantrums. By then we'd gotten through Raymond's head-cracking tantrums and Evelyn's earsplitting shrieking tantrums. We'd survived those; we could survive Ruth's. We decided she won the Academy Award for the most dramatic, loud, physical tantrums. So when she threw one, we all applauded the great performance.

She didn't like that, so she quit throwing her fits.

She also started acting out inappropriately with the other children. We kept her by Domingo's side or mine most of the time to keep an eye on her. She wouldn't listen. We'd give her a task and explain exactly how to do it, and she'd nod like she agreed, and then she'd go and do it in a way that was intentionally destructive. I must confess, I didn't like this little girl at all. I had to keep going to God and asking him to help me love her.

The day came for my appointment with her psychiatrist. The doctor asked me many questions while Ruth sat quietly on the floor, playing with the toys she'd brought with her.

"How is Ruth's behavior? Does she follow the rules?"

"She's wild, mouthy, has no regard for authority, is mean, and has some bad sexual behavior. She steals large amounts of food and eats it all."

"How do you handle that?"

"We have real tight boundaries on her. We don't ever leave her in a room alone with the other children." I paused, thinking. "Other than that we're doing fine."

The psychiatrist tilted her head, tapping her pencil on the top of the file. She stopped herself. "What's her response?"

"She doesn't like being removed from our family activities, so we use that as one of her consequences. As a result, she's trying to make changes to her behavior."

The baffled look in the doctor's eyes as I spoke made me feel a little uneasy. I finally asked, "Am I doing something wrong?"

She leaned forward a little in her chair. "Do you know her history?"

"I'm still waiting for the social worker to tell me. I learn bits and pieces here and there, but nothing substantial." I felt that sense of fear in my gut, knowing I was about to learn about Ruth's past. I knew it was going to break my heart—but I needed to know. "I was told she's supposed to be on medication, but I don't know what for."

"Ruth has been diagnosed with schizophrenia, bipolar disorder, ADHD, obsessive-compulsive disorder ..."

My brain sort of stopped at the word *schizophrenia* and got stuck there.

"Ruth started a fire in her apartment and was abused by her birth father. The medications are to calm her down so her mother can control her." The psychiatrist looked down at Ruth quietly playing next to me. "No one has been able to make her sit and not be destructive. How are you able to get her to be so calm?"

This was so much disturbing information to take in at once. When I finally came back to my senses, I didn't answer her question but asked one of my own: "Why wasn't I told about all this behavior before?"

The doctor took a deep breath. "Probably because no one would take her. She's already been in a foster home for almost two years."

The words of the county worker came back to me—"She is a normal, good little girl."

Now I understood. The county worker had snaked us. She'd called us directly because she knew our agency would've screened Ruth and warned us about her. Pretty smart thinking on the social worker's part. She knew we cared about Mac, so she laid on the guilt trip. Well, hats off to her—we fell for it.

The psychiatrist told me I would need to give Ruth meds right away to control her.

"What would happen if I didn't give her the meds?"

The psychiatrist watched Ruth play and said it was remarkable she listened to me.

I wanted to tell her it was God who helped us with her, but I knew she wouldn't understand. "Could her behavior be because of her mother and what she was exposed to?"

"It's possible," she said.

"Do you think her mother could have made up her behavior or exaggerated it so she didn't have to deal with her?"

"Possibly," she said again.

"Can we try not giving her any meds right now? She's been without for so long, maybe she doesn't need them. If she gets out of control we can put her right back on them."

The doctor thought a moment, then nodded. "Yes. I think that's a good plan."

I felt God put me in favor with her since other doctors weren't always so willing to try something different.

Before we put our kids on meds, we always want to try other things first. For example, one thing we teach our kids is self-control. It's a difficult thing to teach, but our commitment is to do what's best for them, not what's easiest for us. In the long run, self-control helps them in every area of their lives.

When I left the doctor, I asked Ruth why she'd started a fire. Her answer broke my heart. "I was trying to cook because we were hungry!" Just four years old, hungry, and responsible to feed herself and her little brother. It made me wonder how much of what Ruth had done on her lengthy rap sheet was really her fault. Was it because of her circumstances?

But Ruth's behavior went from bad to worse. Not only was she acting out inappropriately, she was trying to engage the other kids in her behavior. She refused to listen.

I finally called the social worker and told her she couldn't live with us any longer. This was the first child we had ever given a seven-day notice on. I felt horrible, but after much prayer we felt it was best for all the kids.

"Please don't send her back," the worker said. "She's done so well in your home. Better than she's done anywhere else."

"That's nice, but we can't keep her. She's too disruptive and harmful for the kids who are now settling in."

"Is there anything I can do to help you keep her? I don't want to see her go to a group home."

"All right." I sighed. "We'll give it one more month."

A few days later I saw her try to kiss a child inappropriately. I got angry, and in a loud voice I said, "Ruth! What are you doing?" Everyone in the room jumped—especially Ruth! I pulled her into the other room. "Pack your clothes. You're leaving."

"Why?"

"What were you thinking? You don't do that—it's inappropriate."

"But, Mom, I was just trying to show her love!"

Oh my goodness! I was hit with a bat once again! Ruth was only trying to show love the way she had been loved!

I needed to sit and regain my thoughts. I was so stunned by

what she'd said. After a few moments I sat her down and spoke to her gently. "Ruth, only married couples kiss each other like that." I then spent a lot of time explaining in detail what is acceptable and what is not. She needed a clear picture of boundaries and what acceptable behavior was for a young girl. I couldn't expect her to live out what she didn't know.

You can see why so many of these young girls who are abused mistake sex for love. But the beauty of this story is our God can heal this mess. We agreed to let Ruth stay with us and take one day at a time.

chapter 19

learning forgiveness

June 2007

Each foster child has a county worker, an agency worker, an adoptions worker (if the child is in the foster-adopt program), and an attorney. Each of these workers came to visit each individual child once a month or more. There were scheduled visits with parents two to three times a week. Sometimes we took the kids to visit with their parents, and sometimes the social workers picked them up. Can you imagine? With five to nine kids in the foster system at one time, it was like we had a revolving door in our home—people in and out all day. We didn't worry about it too much. We had systems for keeping track of who needed to be where and when. It wasn't foolproof, but it worked reasonably well. It kept chaos at bay—as much as is possible in a home like ours.

Tony's worker showed up again, unannounced, only this time I wasn't home. Earlier that day Mac's worker had taken him on a visit with his mother. When he came back, he had a bump on his head.

This big guy was still learning to walk and wasn't steady on his feet. He always seemed to be falling on his head, probably because it was a bit out of proportion with the rest of his body.

Tony's worker looked at Mac and said, "What happened to him?"

Domingo, who is always straightforward, said, "He went on a visit and came back with a bump on his head."

"Did you fill out an accident report?"

He looked at her curiously. "No."

The worker seemed to get agitated and upset.

"It wasn't on my watch," Domingo said.

The rules require any accidents to be reported by the adult who was in charge of the child at the time. Since neither of us was with Mac when he got the bump, there was no way we could fill out a report anyway. That was the responsibility of the social worker who had taken him to and from his visit.

However, this worker apparently wasn't satisfied with Domingo's answer, because everything went downhill after that visit.

Later that day, we were having a meeting with two adoptions workers and were expecting two more to arrive soon. In the middle of this, a supervisor came to the door, wanting to investigate the bump on Mac's head. Domingo took the supervisor to Mac's room, showed him the bump, and explained Mac's developmental delays. He also showed the supervisor that Mac's protruding forehead made the bump look worse than it actually was. The supervisor didn't seem concerned and left.

On the other hand, it was clear Tony's social worker didn't like us. She wanted Tony to leave our home and wouldn't let up. A few days after she threw a stink about the bump on Mac's head, she showed up again—with the county supervisor.

When they arrived, Domingo was outside, holding Mac while watching the other kids play. Because Mac didn't balance well, Domingo buckled him into a chair swing so he could keep an eye on him while talking with the visitors.

As Domingo was talking to the supervisor, he saw Tony's worker taking Mac out of the swing. Before Domingo could say anything, she'd pulled him out and set him on his feet on the ground. Mac tried to take a couple of steps, then *boom!* he fell and *bang!* he got hit in the face by Rose, who was in full swing right next to him.

Domingo rushed to pick up the boy and said, "What are you doing? I put him in there to be safe. You had no business taking him out without asking me."

Mac almost instantly developed a goose egg where he'd been hit. My husband looked at the supervisor and said, "You see what I was telling you about him not being stable on his feet?" I'm sure they got out of there pretty quickly. And the funny thing is, the social worker never filled out an accident report.

This worker was new and young, and I think she believed she had it all figured out. If she could find fault in us, she could get Tony back to his family and be a hero. She wanted this so badly that she arranged for a meeting with Tony's attorney and the judge.

What was wrong with this worker? I wondered. We weren't trying to take this boy away from a family who really wanted him. Reunification had been attempted more than once. Of the families who had had him and given him back, some were relatives. Tony had been in the system for two and a half years before he was placed with us. So it baffled me why the social worker was so insistent that she needed to take him from the only family who had wanted to keep him. There was a point when I was so frustrated with this woman that I thought, *Take him. I really don't care.*

But I did care. Very much. And times like this, I knew Domingo and I were following the Spirit. Who in their right minds would fight so hard to keep a difficult boy, especially when others are fighting to take him back? It had to be that we were following something supernatural.

When a child is brought into a foster home, the foster parents must wait six months before pursuing adoption. However, since Tony's case had been transferred to the adoptions section a while before, we could start adoption procedures immediately. Despite this woman's false accusations, we pressed forward with the help of the adoptions office. They hired an attorney to fight on our behalf. And within a few months, Tony became a Garcia.

With a tremendous smile, he still says to anyone who will listen, "We Garcias stick together."

I still struggle with fear of many things, including the fear that someone will come take our kids. The sad thing is, I know fear is the opposite of trust, and I want to trust fully in God's care, provision, and plans. When there is no calamity in our lives, I fear something bad is going to happen at any minute. When trials do come, I shake in my boots, fearing the worst outcome. Reading the Old Testament helps me; I think of how God rescued the Israelites and took them out of bondage. In the process, his beloved people were privileged to see God's miracles. Yet how quickly they forgot them. They were taken out of bondage from Egypt only to put themselves back in bondage again because of their fear and lack of trust.

At times I'm just like them and let fear get the best of me even though I have seen God part the Red Sea. My God has always been there, has always been trustworthy. He has answered one prayer after another, yet I still fail to trust him.

Trust for me is like a weak muscle. I need to exercise it. So I go to God's Word and fill my mind with God's truth. Then I meditate on it until my fear is gone and I trust God to take care of me. Psalm 34 is a passage in Scripture that puts me on the right track. Verses 4–5 say, "I prayed to the LORD, and he answered me. He freed me from all my fears. Those who look to him for help will be radiant with joy; no shadow of shame will darken their faces."

I have to continually remind myself that I don't need to be afraid of what people say or do. My God is my defender. As long as I obey God, I can trust and fear not! Fear can be my friend when it keeps me on the right track. But it can easily become my enemy when it takes over and I no longer trust the one who knows best. God gave us Tony to teach us this most valuable lesson. God is always there. I just need to call on him.

court

I suppose that time wouldn't have been so hard if those had been the only accusations. But it seemed as though we were continually being attacked; accusations were flying at us from all fronts. Spiritual warfare raged around us, sending us to prayer and fasting. I tried to live the cliché: take one day—sometimes one moment—at a time. But I was exhausted.

You would think parents would be grateful to us for caring for and loving their children in their absence. Instead, we became the enemy. They seemed to forget that the kids were brought to us because of their neglect or child-endangerment issues. We didn't go looking for kids to hijack from their parents.

I was cleaning house with a couple of the older girls and Esther when two social workers showed up at our house—one was the director of our agency, and the other woman looked familiar. This was trouble, and I knew it. Not only was my belly rumbling, it was erupting. We were being investigated again. This time the girls' mom said I had abused the girls. She had photographic proof that I had burned Rose with cigarettes.

I said hello to both of the social workers and let them in. The woman I had recognized was someone from licensing who knew me. I had shared our family's story with her while doing her hair once, so she already knew my heart. How good of God to have sent her to me! I could tell she didn't feel comfortable with the investigation, but she had to do it. She took out pictures the mom had supposedly taken during a visit. I almost laughed when she showed them to me. The photos had cut off the head of the person with the marks. It could have been anyone. The burns could have been photoshopped. I didn't even smoke. It was ridiculous. Still, I brought out Rose so they could check her and verify that there were no marks on her.

The girls' grandmother also claimed I abused the girls. The investigator for that allegation also happened to be a client of mine. She did her job and followed through by speaking to the girls, who refuted what Grandma claimed.

Because the allegations were false, it didn't really matter whether I knew the investigators, but I felt that God was taking care of me, knowing that these awful accusations would be easier for me to face if the investigators were people I knew.

Because the girls' mom despised us, she tried every way she could to destroy us. She continually dredged up something to call the county about. Sometimes it was about stupid things. She claimed we told the girls they must call us "Mom and Dad." When any child came into our home, we told them to call us what our grandchildren did: Mimi and Papi. It usually didn't take long before they chose to call us Mom and Dad, possibly because they heard George and the other kids calling us that. Or possibly because kids really need people to call Mom and Dad.

My husband and I didn't take in these girls with the intention of adopting them, but when they were put into the adoption system, we had to make a choice. Then, when the girls asked us to adopt them, what could we say?

These girls felt safe with us. That wasn't our fault, nor was it a sin. And the more we learned about the children of meth users, the more we understood their need for safety. These kids suffer beyond our imagination and cling to love and safety when they find it. It makes sense that they wouldn't want to go back to that scary environment.

Sometimes the mom's claims were more serious. And each time she called, the agency had to do an investigation.

A hatred for the girls' mother started churning in my soul. I defended it as a righteous hatred. After all, I was caring for and defending the weak. But God has a way of not letting me sit in an unholy place like that for long. Soon I knew in my heart I couldn't be consumed with such hate. God had created this woman—and he loved her too.

I learned that her own mother was an addict, so she had started taking drugs at a young age. She hid from her father. If he couldn't find her, he couldn't hurt her. Like the kids we had taken in, she had been a child who was a victim of the sins of her parents. Only she didn't have someone to give her a way out of her messy home. She wasn't one of the fortunate ones.

psychologist

The agency recommended that the mom and I go to a child psychologist to see if we could mend something. In the days before the appointment, I felt more and more nervous. I prayed I could show my love to this woman as well as convince her that the lies she believed about us weren't true. I hoped that in talking with each other we could both do what was best for the girls. Well, the meeting didn't go at all the way I'd hoped.

This woman was incredibly narcissistic. Everything was about her. She was the victim, blaming everyone else for her bad choices. This was all a conspiracy—everyone in the system was out to get her. After all, she was a good mom who loved her children. When she said, "I really am a good mom," the psychologist responded, "If you were such a good mom, why were your kids taken away from you?"

She often shifted the blame to me, kept making it sound like I was doing all these crazy things. My responses weren't exactly kind. When I tried to explain, she wouldn't hear any of it. I finally told her the girls didn't want to see her and that was because of her, not me.

I went to the meeting wanting to show her the love of Christ, but I'm afraid I showed no love. In fact, I'm sure my anger was far more evident.

attorney knows best

The attorney for the girls had been representing them for two years. She was assigned to decide their fate, but she had never spoken to them and didn't even know what they looked like. And yet she felt that it was in their best interest to send them back to their parents. Most attorneys who work for the courts want reconciliation, and I understood that. But I never understood how these attorneys could have no interest in meeting the kids they represented. How can someone not take into account the input of the foster parents, who are with these children 24-7, who see their pain and anguish as well as their reactions to seeing their parents?

In court, it seemed like everyone had an attorney. One for the stepdad, one for the dad, one for the mom, and the state attorney for the kids. The questions were endless as each of the attorneys had their turn with me, one after the other. They ripped me apart and turned every action of mine into something with an evil-minded motive while trying to portray both of the incarcerated parents as model citizens. This woman who had harmed a child, spent many years locked up, and was *still* in jail (she hoped to get custody of the girls when she was released) was being portrayed as a wonderful person. And we, who were trying to take good care of the girls, were painted as criminals. It made no sense and was so difficult to deal with. Why was I put on trial instead of the parents? The whole fight was so difficult that I was ready to give up and let the girls go back to the mom. But I'd take one look at them and then put my hand in God's for more strength to keep going. It was a horrible place to be and one of the biggest trials I have ever been through.

In our defense, the social worker brought as evidence the video from the police station where the mom told the girls their caregivers would torture and kill them. I brought my detailed journals I kept on all the children, where I wrote what people said verbatim. Since their mom was pulling accusations out of her imagination, she had nothing to back them up. But because she was the mother, her words carried more weight than mine and could have been very damning if I hadn't had the journals; they are what saved us.

To add to the mess, Rose's dad (not Elaine and Evelyn's dad) had been released from prison and was also fighting for custody. Because of the mom's prior convictions, there was a good chance the judge wouldn't decide in her favor, so the dad had decided to divorce her in order to improve his chances.

When there's a fight for what's right, a fight to protect children, I can be strong and stubborn. As a result, we did not make life easy for many social workers and attorneys. But life wasn't easy for us, either. We were on an emotional roller coaster. One thing I can share with wholehearted confidence is that we were never alone. God was always there in our midst. We prayed we would find favor in the courts and with all the workers. And that God would change the parents' hearts—and ours. Our sweet God did just that ... just not right away.

bittersweet

We were about four years into the reunification or adoption process with the girls when we got a call from Elaine and Evelyn's dad. He told us he realized the girls were very attached to us and he didn't want to split up the girls by taking Evelyn and Elaine away from Rose. Also, by then, the girls had lived with us longer than they had with him. He was going to sign the papers and relinquish his rights so we could adopt them.

It was a bittersweet moment for us. I know this was a hard decision for him. Unlike their mom, he was putting the girls' needs before his. I felt a great sense of compassion for him. We'd had enough contact with him that I knew I loved this man and that he would always be a part of our lives. We told him he was welcome in our home, and he still comes for a visit when he can. The girls now enjoy his company and look forward to the visits. Only God could have changed all of our hearts. God changed this man's heart to relinquish the girls, and ours to accept him as part of our lives.

Mom, however, didn't give up. She continued to appeal the court's decision. In the end, it was one of the longest and hardest cases that court had ever heard. From the time Elaine and Evelyn entered our home until they were adopted was an eternal span of four years. Mom received a restraining order—for eight years she was not supposed to be around children unsupervised and she was to have no contact with us.

forgiveness

Elaine had prayed with me to receive Christ about a year after she arrived, when she was upset about the jail visit. She had this pure and simple faith and just trusted and believed. Since then she had been praying a lot for their mom to let Rose be adopted. Not long before Elaine's adoption was to become final, I went into her room and found her crying.

I sat on the bed next to her. "What's wrong?"

She slowed her tears enough to say, "I'm going back to my mom."

"Elaine, why would you say that? You're going to be adopted soon!"

"I can't let Rose go back to her. I have to go with her to protect her. My mother is awful." A list of things her mom had done tumbled out of her mouth.

I was astounded. Knowing how much this girl despised and feared her mother, I couldn't believe she would sacrifice what she obviously loved—this family and her own safety—for her sister.

She looked up at me, her eyes red. "Why isn't God helping?"

"He is. We just can't see it right now. You need to have faith." I gently took her chin in my hand so I could tilt her face to look into my eyes. "God never said life would be fair."

"I hate her."

"I can understand." Boy, I understood. I hated her too. I felt her abuse to the boy she had taken and to the girls was unforgivable. "You've suffered a lot, and you've seen your sisters suffer too. But your anger is putting you in bondage. You've got to forgive your mother. Until you forgive her, you won't be free."

The look on her face said she didn't understand.

"Forgiving her will help you heal."

"Okay, Mom. I'll try." She cried, and we prayed together. I encouraged her to also pray for God to change her mom's heart.

When I walked out of the room, shame washed over me. Here I was asking Elaine to forgive her mother, but I hadn't forgiven her. I was harboring my own hatred for her. As a matter of fact, I hated most of the parents of our kids, refusing to forgive them. I went to my closet and asked God to forgive me for my hatred and to soften my calloused heart. He reminded me that these were lost and broken people, just as I was.

Jesus was beaten, tortured, and spit on, and then he suffered a horrific death to pay for the sins of the world. Who do I think I am that I can choose who deserves my forgiveness? Shame on me!

I have often pondered the time when Jesus washed the disciples' feet. He knew Judas was his enemy and was going to betray him in a few hours, yet he included him in his humble act of love and service. This is the example I decided to follow.

I went back to Elaine and said, "Elaine, I have to tell you that I haven't forgiven your mom either. I asked God to forgive me for my attitude and to help me forgive her."

Instead of me teaching Elaine about forgiveness, God used Elaine to teach me.

chapter 20

adoption

National Adoption Day, November 2008

The happy day finally came. The judge had ruled in our favor! Elaine and Evelyn were going to be ours. We were like the Israelites when God parted the Red Sea, and we danced and rejoiced over what God had done.

The girls' mom had gotten out of jail and had been transferred to a rehabilitation center, still hoping to get Rose. Elaine was still very concerned about this and would go into her room and pray about the situation. She struggled to forgive her mom and didn't want her near Rose.

The day came not long after when Rose was also relinquished to us. It was like a ton of weight was taken off our shoulders. As I reflect on those difficult times, I praise God, realizing he gave us the grace when we needed it. Our God protected us, gave us wisdom when we asked for it, and never left us alone. Yet, in the midst of all our excitement, an inexplicable weight settled on my heart. How could I really rejoice in the separation of a mother and her daughters? I knew that while we were rejoicing, the mom was mourning the loss of her three girls. When I was in the thick of the battle, my automatic reflex was to fight. Did I really win?

Not long before the adoption was to be finalized, we were asked whether we wanted an open adoption or a closed one. Would it be okay for the mom to visit the girls? We didn't even think twice—we wanted it closed. She was really upset with our decision. *You know what?* I thought. *That's what you get for being so mean and wicked.*

Whammo! God laid immediate conviction on me, and a verse popped into my head: "Love your enemies and pray for those who persecute you" (Matt. 5:44 NIV). I had to confess my sin and ask God what he wanted me to do. The answer? Give her my email address and maybe send pictures once in a while.

Elaine flipped. She didn't want her mother to have any information about her—especially pictures. She feared her mom would find her and take her away. She had a recurring nightmare that she and I were walking, when suddenly her mom came up behind us and pulled out the knife she always carried. Then I disappeared, and Elaine knew I was dead.

I had to be careful and respect my daughter's feelings. So for a while I didn't give her mother any information about Elaine. When she asked, I told her why, and it made her very upset. Trying not to sound mean, I wrote, "That's between you and Elaine. I've made a promise to her. She's the one I need to be loyal to, not you."

One morning we got a call from our adoptions worker. He asked us if we would consider waiting to finalize our adoption of the girls until National Adoption Day. They wanted us to be the featured family. We agreed since it required us to wait only one more week for the adoptions to be final.

We had no idea how much media would be there, nor that they were going to do a televised interview with the two older girls. I felt uneasy about it, but Domingo thought we needed to share what a blessing adoption was and encourage those who would listen to consider it. What we didn't know was that CBS shared the story with other stations so it wasn't only local; it was also broadcast on their Sacramento news program. The girls shared that they were happy and loved and that they had lots of brothers and sisters.

Even though by now I was in contact with their mother via email, we had never told her the exact date of their adoptions being finalized.

When we got home (after our celebratory stop at Denny's), I checked my email and saw a message from the mom. "I was at my aunt's house and the TV was on. I saw my kids being adopted and it was so hard."

It felt strange to console this woman I struggled to forgive. "You know, I'm really sorry that you had to see that," I wrote. The moment I'd typed the words, I realized I was beginning to love my enemy. I felt sorry for this woman. She hadn't seen her girls in four years, and then to see them on TV, becoming part of someone else's family …

Her emails were usually pleasant, and I shared that we loved her girls and that we would always care for them. And surprisingly, I started enjoying the emails from her. She would share photos and stories about the girls when they were little.

Yes, it was her fault the girls were taken away, but I needed to encourage her. Can you imagine? Here I was, trying to comfort a mother who had lost her children to me. Only God could have put me in that unique situation. I shared Christ and told her I was sorry for her pain.

Soon she'd had one baby and had another one on the way. After the birth of the second child, I met with her and her husband at a coffeehouse. I was very nervous, but Domingo and I felt that this was what God wanted me to do. I needed to do everything in my power to make peace with this woman. I saw her two babies, and she even put one in my arms. I felt like this was some sort of peacemaking ritual for her, and it touched me.

We still exchange emails, but not as often as we did in the beginning. In her emails now, she thanks me for loving and caring for her girls. I believe she is trying hard, and I'm proud of her and the changes she and her husband have made. If you would have told me back in the middle of the battle that I would learn to love this woman, I would have told you that you were nuts. You see, God answered the prayers I prayed—that he would change the parents' hearts … and ours.

As I sit here, I can hear the sound of angels singing. My angels. Nearly every night while they clean up the kitchen, they sing. "Pie Jesu," "Concrete Angel," and "To Believe." Tiny Rose wowed the church last Christmas with her solo of "Mary, Did You Know?," bringing tears to the eyes of many in the audience. Hearing their amazing voices fills my heart with joy and thankfulness to God, who took three wildcats and turned them into delightful and precious girls.

Mac's and Ruth's adoptions

Mac *loved* Domingo. He idolized him, following him everywhere, watching everything he did, calling him Daddy. It was the only intelligible word he said. He loved tools like Domingo did and quickly learned the names for all of them.

Mac didn't want to be anywhere except by Domingo's side. He hated going to school, kicking and screaming when the bus came to pick him up for his special-ed program. Because he was a foster child, he had to go. He was miserable at school and mean to the other kids. The good news for the teachers was that, because he was so food motivated, it was easy to give him snacks for good behavior. But the reality was he just wanted to be with Domingo.

Ruth, on the other hand, did well in school and loved being there. She and Samantha were in the same classroom. One afternoon Samantha came home and informed me that someone was stealing food from the lunches in the classroom. I immediately suspected Ruth and questioned her. She was such a good liar that I believed her when she said she hadn't touched anyone else's food, and I stood up for her.

A few weeks later, I was cleaning her room and found all kinds of food wrappers in her backpack. Not just a handful, but at least thirty of them! Even though I caught her red-handed, it took hours of questioning before she finally confessed.

I was so embarrassed to go to her teacher and tell her that my daughter was the lunch bandito. It wasn't easy to humble myself like that.

So although Ruth was doing better, we still didn't know if she was a child we could handle. Visits with their birth mom brought out all kinds of anxiety and issues in both of the kids. Mac didn't want to go on the visits in the first place, throwing tantrums that his mom didn't know how to handle. Ruth demanded all the attention, causing a power struggle between her and Mac. Afterward, Ruth acted out, causing even more chaos at home.

After two years in our home, the day came for the mom to appear in court. The social worker told me she (the social worker) was going to ask the judge to put the kids into adoptions. Would we consider adopting them if she did that?

Oh, I was really uncertain about these kids. We loved Mac, but we knew we would lose him if Ruth left. I knew God had brought this girl to us, but I was very hesitant about committing to adoption. I'd never felt this way with the other kids. I had always been willing to help any child, but this one scared me.

In court, the social worker recommended the kids be placed in adoptive placement. No judgment was made at that time since the mom would appeal the decision at a later date. However, the kids were still going to be put into the foster-adopt program. This meant Domingo and I had to decide what we were going to do. If we weren't going to adopt these two, they needed to go to a home that would.

Lord, what do you want us to do?

Because of the difficulty that Ruth brought and the fact that Mac would need special care for the rest of his life, I needed to be absolutely sure that adopting these kids was the right decision. Also, after four years of court with the girls and many false allegations against us by workers and parents, I was exhausted, running on empty.

That night Domingo and I decided to fast and pray for God to give us a specific answer, to make it very clear about whether we should adopt these kids. My prayers were that if God wanted us to adopt them, we wouldn't have to endure another long, drawn-out court battle—that it would happen quickly and it would be clear that their mom should not have them.

The next morning the kids' social worker called. "Irene," she said, "you are not going to believe what just happened."

The birth mom had just been in her office to tell her she was not going to fight for the kids in court. She wanted to sign the kids over to us because she felt she couldn't care for them and would likely harm them again. They wouldn't be safe with her, and she knew it.

Well, I about dropped the phone. When I prayed, I really didn't expect such a quick and clear answer. Why do I keep doubting God? You'd think I'd get it by now. God has our back. God cares about us and these kids.

After the very specific answer to our very specific prayers, we knew that whatever struggles and issues we would have with Ruth, we could never look back and say, "Why did we adopt her?" Instead, I will say, "Lord, show me what we should do." No matter what trials would come, we would be able to endure them with confidence, knowing that God assigned these children to our family and that any trials will be used by God to perfect us and to draw us closer to him. He will never give us a task we cannot accomplish through his mighty power. We know for certain God will give us the ability to care for these kids.

It has been two years since we adopted these kids, and they have grown by leaps and bounds. We pulled Mac out of school because he continued to scream in terror every time the bus came to pick him up. We felt it was detrimental to him. He needed to bond with us and know I was his mom. For six months I tried to teach him the basics—ABC and 123. He simply wasn't able to learn. I was so discouraged that I almost put him back in school. I prayed and prayed for our little boy, and God intervened. Now he is learning. In 2012 he started talking. As of the writing of this book, he knows all his alphabet and can count to thirty on his own. He has read his first book too. And talk? Oh my. Sometimes you can't stop the flow of all his words—he even talks to guests without hesitation.

Ruth has had many struggles, but she loves her family and tries really hard to do the right thing. She and her brother still struggle with food issues, but she knows she needs to change. She has the gift of serving, and we praise her all the time for that, telling her it pleases God when she serves. She glows when Domingo kisses her. I can't imagine our lives without this girl. I have fallen madly in love with Ruth. Once again, through the power of God.

Once the kids were adopted, we realized all of them would do better in a situation where each of their special needs could be taken into consideration. We also believed that it was our responsibility to train and educate them ourselves. So we built a schoolroom and decided to homeschool all the kids. I admit this is the hardest thing Domingo and I have ever done. We don't feel qualified, but we have committed to give it our all and to do it to the glory of God.

When I look at Ruth and Mac, I think of God's specific answer to my specific prayer. When God does this, my soul is overjoyed, feeling as though we can conquer any obstacle that is in front of us. I tell my little ones they have superpowers and can conquer the highest mountains—through the power of God.

chapter 21

the sheep and the goats

*Pure and genuine religion in the sight of God the
Father means caring for orphans and widows in their
distress and refusing to let the world corrupt you.*

James 1:27

The number of kids in world who currently need a home is over one hundred million.[1] In the United States, children in foster care are nearly four times more likely to commit suicide than other children.[2] Fifty-nine percent of juveniles arrested for prostitution in Los Angeles County were in the foster care system.[3] Sixty-six percent will be homeless, go to jail, or die within one year of leaving the foster care system at eighteen.[4] This is more than tragic. It's shameful in a country like ours.

We feel it's time for us to become more vocal about what we believe to be the mandate from God in James 1:27. The verse tells us that we are expected to visit the orphans and widows with the intent of meeting their needs. And what does an orphan need most? A mom and a dad.

People have asked how we could have made such serious decisions about children so quickly over the phone, without praying about whether we should let more kids come into our home. When God says, "Don't murder or steal," I don't have to pray about whether I should be involved in those things, because I already know his will. In the same way, God says in his Word that we should take care of the widows and orphans. I don't have to pray to know if this is his will because he already told me it is. He wants us to do it. Period. And Domingo and I felt that as long as God kept bringing us kids, and we had room, we would keep taking them in.

In Matthew 25:31–46, Jesus talked about the end of time, when all the nations will gather at the throne of King Jesus, and he will separate the people as a shepherd separates the sheep from the goats. The King welcomes the sheep into the kingdom and sends the goats to eternal fire.

The sheep are the ones who took care of his needs whether he was hungry, thirsty, in prison, or needing clothing or a place to sleep. The goats neglected his needs.

Each group questions the King. When was he hungry? Thirsty? When was he in need? To the goats he says, "I tell you the truth, when you refused to help the least of these my brothers and sisters, you were refusing to help me" (v. 45).

To the sheep the King says, "I tell you the truth, when you did it to one of the least of these my brothers and sisters, you were doing it to me!" (v. 40).

We felt "the least of these" included orphans and kids in the foster care system. If it does, and the church is ignoring them in their need, then the church is in real trouble. Certainly many churches are eager to help the lost and the orphans in other countries, but what about those in our own neighborhoods? Aren't we told to love our neighbors as ourselves? Jesus didn't *command* you to love yourself; you do that automatically. You eat when you're hungry, you sleep when you're tired, and you keep your body clothed and groomed. The command is to love your *neighbor* in the same way that you care for yourself.

These kids are our neighbors, and they need food, beds, and people to clothe them and parent them. We should automatically be caring for them and meeting their needs.

As you can see from the statistics, a staggering number of children in our country are in this situation and need moms and dads. Sending money and giving food or clothing are good things, but I challenge you to do more. Why not give a lifetime commitment? Isn't God's commitment to us for a lifetime?

church programs

Our churches have programs for everything. There are programs for recovery, divorce, widows. There are programs for children from birth through high school. Then there are the ones for men, women, family, marriage, parenting, singles, college, and career. Don't forget the plethora of activities for fellowship and evangelism. It seems as though there's always a Bible study series or class to help us enhance our Christianity.

However, there's trouble in the church. The divorce rate is up, as well as the number of members struggling with alcohol, drugs, and pornography. Many people in the church are on antidepressants

because they can't cope. The family is falling apart—dads aren't leading and moms aren't following, and the kids are walking away from
their faith. With all these great programs, why is the church having
such a hard time?

If we stopped all these programs that help us focus on ourselves
and followed the Spirit's leading instead, what would happen? I
believe we would be walking in "love, joy, peace, patience, kindness,
goodness, faithfulness, gentleness, and self-control" (Gal. 5:22–23).
It's when the flesh leads us by our passions and desires that we are
blinded by a veil of self-centeredness. Galatians 5:19–21 says, "When
you follow the desires of your sinful nature, the results are very clear:
sexual immorality, impurity, lustful pleasures, idolatry, sorcery,
hostility, quarreling, jealousy, outbursts of anger, selfish ambition,
dissension, division, envy, drunkenness, wild parties, and other sins
like these. Let me tell you again, as I have before, that anyone living
that sort of life will not inherit the Kingdom of God."

If we were to follow the Spirit, I believe not only would we not
need all the programs we have, but we would be automatically taking
care of the needy—including the orphans.

I think of the thousands of parents who are involved in parenting
classes, hoping to create the perfect family by training their children
to become obedient and Christlike. Think of how quickly their children would learn by example if they took in a child to show him or
her the love of Christ. This could be the greatest gift you as a parent
ever give your birth children—for them to see your Christianity in
action.

And don't you want to see God take a few loaves of bread and a
couple of fish and feed the five thousand? Then step out in faith and

take in a child or two. It will be an adventure you will never forget. Stepping out in faith brings us closer to God and puts us in a front-row seat to watch him in action.

the challenge

We are honored, privileged, and blessed to live in this country. And we are thankful that it has programs and systems in place to take care of the orphans. We know it's not perfect, but nevertheless we thank God for it. We have worked with many social workers who labored long and hard hours on behalf of the kids. We admit that there were times we didn't agree with the system or some of the workers. But God always intervened and changed our hearts or theirs. Our family is filled with gratitude for those many workers who stood behind our family and helped us navigate the maze of the system.

However, we know many workers who have seen so much child abuse they've had to walk away from their jobs because they couldn't handle it anymore. We know workers who are burned out because of their heavy caseloads. If the church were more involved in taking in children from the foster system, these workers wouldn't have such heavy caseloads because there wouldn't be as many kids who needed help.

We do want to acknowledge and thank the many foster parents who truly seek the best for the children they care for. God bless those who labor so hard on behalf of the kids. They all desperately need your prayers—the workers and the foster parents as well as the system.

We would take in more children, but we're full! The county says we're maxed out and will not give us any more. We trust that if God

262   rich in love

has other children for us, he'll make a way. Domingo and I turned sixty a year ago, so we don't have a whole lot of time left, but God knows our time clock and will provide accordingly.

We continually share with our children that as a family we need to help the needy—especially widows—and we do. We are teaching our children by practice and example that when God puts a need in front of us, it's our responsibility to follow through.

In the end, one thing is for certain—we will all stand before God as he sits on his holy throne. There will be two lines—one for the sheep (those who took care of the needs of "the least of these") and one for the goats (those who did not). If you died today, which line would you be standing in? Which line do you *want* to be in? I don't know about you, but I want to be in the middle of a bunch of woolly sheep.

conclusion

What does it take to raise foster kids? Two dummies and a Bible.

As I come to the ending of this book, I realize how very rich in love my husband and I are. I think of how God, in his beautiful grace, took these two naive young kids and tucked them under his wings. How he brought us to our knees and revealed his will and purpose for our lives, gently guiding us and then forgiving us when we got in his way. So many times we took his hand and held on so tightly, afraid to let go. Then he gently released us and showed us he would never give us a task we couldn't accomplish with his help.

For these past few months, I have had to go back in time and remember things I had locked deep in the vault of my heart. I must confess it was difficult for me to write about the events in our distant past and to relive many of the things I had chosen to forget. After all, these things are *past*. We are so different now.

One night I read Domingo the part of the story about when we got married. As I got to the part where I wanted to go home because I was homesick, I started to cry. Domingo reached over, put his hand on me, and said tenderly, "Irene, you were just a little girl." Yes, we were so young, and our lives were chaos because there was no God in them.

When Domingo and I talk about our salvation, we always share our past. But we've never talked intimately about the pain we both suffered. So in writing this book, we have had to look at and face the demons from our past, unearthing some of the things we had buried for a reason. Thankfully, this hard work was a healing process for us. We both thank our Father for forgiving us, stepping into our lives, and leading us forward.

Those were the trials God gave me so that he could perfect me. And the more I have grown, the more I have learned God will never give me more than I can handle. There will always be trials in my life, but my sweet Jesus will hold my hand through them. Sometimes I forget that even my marriage can be a trial that perfects me, and then I remember that my troubled marriage taught me about forgiveness, love, and humility.

Many have asked why I stayed in the marriage. I really can't answer why, because it's too complicated—even for me to understand. What I know is I wouldn't change a thing if that's what it took for me to be where I am today. After all, now I'm married to an amazing man. He is the godliest man I know. When God called him, Domingo did a 180-degree turn and never looked back. My husband is selfless and compassionate to orphans. When he speaks, you can hear the love and passion in his voice for these helpless children. So I praise God for these forty-five years of marriage to the same boy. Think of all I would have missed had I not stayed!

I pray that as a result of revealing some of the more shameful and broken areas of our lives, this book will touch many broken hearts and give hope to many who suffer. Our God spoke the universe into existence; he can fix any broken relationship or broken heart.

life in the Garcia household

Life in the Garcia household can be crazy hectic or quiet with bodies and pillows all over the floor as the kids watch a movie. Domingo has initiated Movie Night, which includes all the junk food the kids wish they could eat during the week but aren't allowed to. Popcorn, soda from the soda machine a client gave us for Christmas, and sometimes ice-cream sundaes or candy. I can tell you, these kids love Friday nights!

For their birthdays, each child gets to pick out what he or she wants for dinner and dessert—pizza is often the food of choice. And we have a lot of birthdays in our house. There's always someone or something to celebrate.

During the week, Domingo teaches both the younger kids and the older kids from the Bible. The older kids study deep topics from the Word on their own, then Domingo asks tough questions when they gather for the official study. They are assigned memory verses and receive a small candy bar as a reward if they can say them. The older kids also participate in the simpler Bible study Domingo has for the younger ones. Every child has a memory verse that's appropriate for his or her age or intellectual level. And to help the squirming, squiggling kids stay on task a little better, they each get a small pile of some sort of crunchy treat like Cheetos to munch on while they study.

School begins at 7:00 each morning during the school year. Domingo is in charge of math and science, I take care of

English—reading and writing—and we share history. The kids also have supplemental classes at a local school. In church they either attend Sunday school or help out in another class a younger sibling is in.

Our garage has been transformed into a playroom for all ages. There's a pool table, workout equipment—including a treadmill—and television for approved movies and educational video games only. For example, the kids are learning all about the animals of the world through an animal Monopoly game. If you open a large, homemade wooden box near the garage door, you'll find a massive tangle of tennis shoes. Dig through them, and you're likely to find a pair that fits you—if you can find its mate.

Outside, Domingo has created a haven for kids. There are three trampolines and a bouncy playground thing that looks like a plane and seats six kids (or a few kids and one crazy adult). In the center of it all is a three-story clubhouse that is every kid's dream. On the second floor (which can be reached only by a ladder) is a room with fold-down bunks for sleepovers. There's also a minimicrowave for popcorn, a minifridge for cold drinks, and an old cast-off TV set on which to play Xbox games. The third floor can be reached only by a knotted rope so the kids can learn more motor skills. Up on the third floor are some old baby car seats. Domingo discovered they are perfect for young boys who want to hang out and play games or pretend.

On the other side of the house, Domingo has built a long, three-sided shed that houses the many bicycles (ten!) our family owns. Each bicycle slot has a wooden knob above it for the bike helmet to hang on. Now, whether the bikes actually make it into the shed is another story....

Beyond that is Domingo's shop—which he wisely ordered larger than he thought he'd need for all his tools and equipment for repairing cars and building things. Also housed in the shop are our dirt bikes. Since our boat was the only item we couldn't sell when we moved north, we decided that perhaps God was encouraging us to keep it. And it has been a joy. There are a number of lakes not too far from our home, and we have spent many a lazy summer's day hanging out on the boat or zipping around the lake, dragging some sort of inflatable water toy with shrieking children clinging to it.

All over our wooded three acres are places for kids to hide, imagine, climb, and ride bikes over dirt trails. (Can you tell Domingo never stops?)

Domingo and I are excited for this journey we are on. Our kids have had so many obstacles and disabilities that for a long time all we could do was use our energy to try to stay afloat. We have been working hard training and schooling our children and trying to get the new stuff in their little hearts and get the old stuff out. We can see God's work in this, especially when folks come over and can't believe these are the troubled children who came to live with us. Only God can do something like that.

2013

Now that you've heard the stories, I'm sure you wonder where the kids are today.

Our two oldest boys have grown up sharing us with many other children. We are thankful they embraced their brothers and sisters, then followed us in the same journey with their own families, each of them adopting children and teaching them that no matter where they came from, all are loved equally. Both of them have endured many trials, but they know God is waiting for them at the finish line.

Esther has encountered many obstacles in her life, but she is learning to conquer her weaknesses. When the men in our church built our addition, they gave her a beautiful room with her own bathroom and deck. She is my right-hand helper. She does so much for all of us. God gifted her with hospitality. This girl can cook! We enjoy her many food creations and her delicious baked goodies. When my kids want cookies or sweets, she whips them up like it's nothing. We could have never taken in so many kids without Esther always joyfully working in the background.

Alfred is living in Southern California. He cares for my ninety-one-year-old father, who is suffering from Parkinson's disease and dementia. Alfred is so kind and tender to him. We are grateful for his gift of compassion.

Marie is now in her final phase of nursing school. If all goes well, she will graduate next year with her RN degree. It wasn't easy for her, but she persevered despite her learning disabilities.

Vivian is happily married and raising a beautiful family. She has become her family's strong anchor—her focus is raising her kids. She is very involved with them and lays down strong boundaries for her children.

Doreen and Felix have chosen more difficult paths for their lives. But I know it's not over yet. We still pray for them, wanting the best for them.

The younger children still struggle, just like normal children. But they are amazing kids. Among them we have those who are extremely creative; are outstanding jocks; are beautiful, beautiful singers (can knock your socks off); are excellent writers; love music and dance; work hard; have photographic memories; are intellectually gifted; and are just so cute! Our goal is to find their gifts, talents, and strengths, then help them develop and nourish them. We know each child has a different bent, so each one will need to be taught differently. Besides developing their life skills, our ultimate goal is to paint a clear picture of who God is so they will have an understanding of him and love him with all their heart, soul, and might. As they develop a relationship with God, our hope is they will see clearly what their purpose in life is too.

Domingo has been a full-time dad ever since Mac came to us. He is the one who keeps track of the kids' schedules. He takes them to doctor's appointments (and there are many!) and doles out medicine and injections. He loves his kids, and they love him. After dinner, as the girls assigned kitchen chores clean up, he sits in his rocker at the edge of the dining room, kids clustered around him like he's Santa Claus, waiting to hear their deepest wish. Oh, he's such a good dad! He takes the boys on "man trips" to teach them the many skills involved in being a true man of God. He believes in the development of every part of a child. He doesn't focus only on the spiritual or emotional but on the physical aspects as well. He proudly shows photos of his boys, when they were under ten years of age, taking an engine out of a truck while he gave instructions from the sidelines. He taught them well!

God has blessed me with two spheres of influence. At the salon, my role is to be a light to all who come in. I want everyone—from my assistants to clients to sales reps—to hear about the great God I serve and the wonderful things he has done in my life. At home, as mom, I keep the household running by assigning chores for housecleaning, laundry, and kitchen duties. One day a week we girls take a couple of hours to clean house together, singing, laughing, and yes, sometimes grumbling. But we get it done! We love it when the boys go away so we can have girlie time. Whether we're having "piglics" (picnics) on the floor of our living room, talking girl talk, or going on special outings, you can be sure we're going to have a great bonding time.

I find that, still, God uses my children to teach and humble me. I may feel like "big stuff" at the salon because I'm in charge, but at home, I am continually aware of all the places within me that still need growth and change. When we took in kids, I thought it was so God would use us to bless them. Silly me! Yes, they benefited from our love, but God also used them to teach and bless *me*. He uses them to sift and refine me, bringing me closer to him.

Even though Domingo and I are over sixty, we have many years left to raise our younger children to adulthood. We continually pray for good health so we can keep up with them! They are our joy, and we love them very much.

We now have four teens in our home. I must say—this sure makes life an adventure! Soon we will have seven teens! We continually go to one of our favorite verses, James 1:5: "If any of you lacks wisdom, you should ask God, who gives generously to all without finding fault, and it will be given to you" (NIV). How many times has God shown me that his wisdom is all I need? Here is our perfect Father, the one who created us, saying, "I have all the answers. I know the blueprints for each of my children, and I will share those with you. All you need to do is ask."

These last years have been extremely draining as we have been knee-deep in raising our children while trying to figure out each one's bents so we can encourage them as individuals. Every time I felt like I couldn't deal with another issue, a new one arrived. I talked to God alone in my closet, out loud in my car, or quietly in my head about everything—praying without ceasing (1 Thess. 5:17). I long to spend my time alone with my God. I feel like the psalmist who said, "As the deer pants for the water brooks, so my soul pants for You, O God" (Ps. 42:1 NASB). I cannot make it through a day without talking and praying to my Hero, my God, my Father.

Domingo and I pray that we will teach our children all we know and believe about our King so they will walk with him one day. We pray that we will live our lives in obedience and with joy, giving God all the glory. For he who is richest in love has passed those riches on to us so that we can give them to others.

notes

1. "Facts & Statistics," Orphan Hope International, http://www.orphanhopeintl.org/facts-statistics/.

2. Helen Ramaglia, "Suicide and the Foster Child," The Chronicle of Social Change, July 11, 2013, https://chronicleofsocialchange.org/opinion/suicide-and-the-foster-child/3317.

3. Kevin Ryan, "Keeping Foster Kids Safe from Prostitution," *The Blog, Huffington Post,* October 25, 2013, http://www.huffingtonpost.com/kevin-m-ryan/keeping-foster-kids-safe-_b_4159768.html.

4. Brittany Nunn, "Statistics Suggest Bleak Futures for Children Who Grow Up in Foster Care," *Amarillo Globe-News,* June 24, 2012, http://amarillo.com/news/local-news/2012-06-24/what-comes-next.